SKIN IN THE GAME: POOR KIDS AND PATRIOTS

Major General Dennis Laich is a citizen, a soldier, and a patriot. In Skin in the Game, he invites Americans to reflect on this very hard truth: the All-Volunteer Force is a bad bargain. Basic U. S. military policy needs changing. Here is an essential guide on where to begin.

—Andrew J. Bacevich, author of *Breach of Trust: How Americans Failed Their Soldiers and Their Country*

* * * *

In this well written and provocative book, General Laich argues that the All-Volunteer Force is not working. While many people would disagree with his conclusion, this book makes it clear that this nation needs to engage in a dialogue about the lessons we have learned in using an AVF to protect our national security for the past 40 years.

—Lawrence J. Korb
Senior Fellow
Center for American Progress

* * * *

"This book is a must-read for anyone who cares about the future of the US military. Retired Major General Dennis Laich asks whether our All-Volunteer Force is working, whether it is fair, and whether it will serve American national interests in the future. His answers, based on 35 years of hands-on experience, will shock even the most seasoned analysts of military affairs. I highly recommend *Skin in the Game* to anyone who is touched by the US armed forces, which is to say, all Americans."

—Aaron Belkin is author of *Bring Me Men: Military Masculinity and the Benign Facade of American Empire, 1898-2001*

* * * *

As the parent of a Marine who is currently on his second tour in Afghanistan, I found "Skin in the Game-Poor Kids and Patriots" resonated with me on many levels. As a taxpayer, I find General Laich's fiscal arguments regarding sustainability compelling enough on their own to demand a broader dialogue on the effectiveness of the AVF. As a citizen with skin in the game, who has witnessed first hand the high cost paid by military personnel and their families, I find his arguments for fairness and equality of sacrifice to be overwhelming.

—George Knapp, MBA, Met E., Ordinary Citizen and Proud Parent of a Patriot.

* * * *

MG Laich brings an experienced, compassionate and humane voice to a much needed national dialogue over how we staff our armed forces. Drawing on his expertise and wisdom, *Skin in the Game* offers a compelling alternative to the current system--which Laich argues is broken--based on a vision for civil-military relations that's more fair, efficient, and sustainable.

—Nathaniel Frank, author of *Unfriendly Fire: How the Gay Ban Undermines the Military and Weakens America.*

* * * *

General Laich provides an opening in a long overdue dialogue about alternatives to the All Volunteer Force. An essential component of that dialogue is the requirement for equal participation of women citizens as part of the solution.

—MG (Ret.) Gale Pollock, a member of the Defense Advisory Committee on Women in the Services

* * * *

General Dennis Laich is a rabble-rousing patriot of the first order. His "Skin in the Game…Poor Kids and Patriots" is a gimlet-eyed gaze at the U.S. military's all-volunteer force at 40. He details the growing risk of subcontracting out the nation's defense to hired guns representing only 1% of the citizenry, so the rest of America can shop.

—Mark Thompson the Pulitzer Prize winning national security correspondent at TIME Magazine

SKIN IN THE GAME: POOR KIDS AND PATRIOTS

Major General (Ret.) Dennis Laich

*Why shouldn't we ask all our citizens to bear some
responsibility and pay some price? ... Those who are serving
today and dying today are the middle class and lower class.*

—Secretary of Defense (then Senator) Chuck Hagel

iUniverse LLC
Bloomington

Skin in the Game: Poor Kids and Patriots

iUniverse books may be ordered through booksellers or by contacting:

iUniverse
1663 Liberty Drive
Bloomington, IN 47403
www.iuniverse.com
1-800-Authors (1-800-288-4677)

Because of the dynamic nature of the Internet, any web addresses or links contained in this book may have changed since publication and may no longer be valid. The views expressed in this work are solely those of the author and do not necessarily reflect the views of the publisher, and the publisher hereby disclaims any responsibility for them.

Any people depicted in stock imagery provided by Thinkstock are models, and such images are being used for illustrative purposes only.

Certain stock imagery © Thinkstock.

ISBN: 978-1-4917-0382-3 (sc)
ISBN: 978-1-4917-0383-0 (hc)
ISBN: 978-1-4917-0384-7 (e)

Library of Congress Control Number: 2013915048

Printed in the United States of America.

iUniverse rev. date: 10/02/2013

This book is dedicated to the millions of Americans who have chosen to serve their country's all-volunteer force. In particular, it is dedicated to those service members and their families who have served since September 11, 2001. Their service and their sacrifice are remarkable. To a large extent, this is their story. It is also the story of how the remainder of Americans have viewed the military—and the way it is manned—through a lens of fear, apathy, ignorance, and guilt.

CONTENTS

FOREWORD

One of the hallmarks of a vibrant democracy is the willingness of its citizens and its leaders to confront difficult problems. This activity requires fact-based dialogue that largely excludes self-interest, partisan politics, and ideology. Today our nation is faced with a host of difficult problems that we seem unable to effectively confront: immigration reform, budget deficits, unemployment, and climate change, and more. Our track record in addressing these problems is poor as Congress' approval rating hovers near single digits and American citizens become more frustrated and divided. Within this context, Skin in the Game posits some important questions about the effectiveness and viability of the All-Volunteer Force.

On July 1 of this year the fortieth anniversary of the All-Volunteer Force passed virtually unnoticed; no parades, no rallies, no conferences, and very few editorials lauding or criticizing the method by which we fill the ranks of our military. The All-Volunteer Force has had a profound effect on our national security, our budget deficits, and our social fabric. We have come to accept a volunteer military as two generations of Americans have never been required to serve in the defense of their nation or their liberties. That task has fallen predominantly on those in the lower and middle classes while the wealthy and well-connected pursue other activities. We hail the heroics and sacrifices of those who serve and their families, and call all of them "heroes". For the most part, we collectively look away from the consequences of their service:

posttraumatic stress disorder, drug and alcohol abuse, suicide, and homelessness, to say nothing of combat casualties and serious injuries. All of these consequences are borne by one percent of our population while the other ninety nine percent go about their lives. This book raises serious questions about the fairness, efficiency, and sustainability of the All-Volunteer Force in the future.

Neither recruiters in our hometowns nor senior officials at the Pentagon can adequately address this issue. While no current crisis compels us to derive suitable solutions today, the problem of how we man our armed forces in the future must be a dialogue that we all share now. Waiting until a crisis appears on our doorstep may limit our options in confronting real threats to our national security. This book offers a framework to begin the conversation, engage the real issues without prejudice, and serves as a clarion call to avoid potentially disastrous circumstances in the future. Certainly the question we want to avoid is "what if we had a war and no one showed up on our side?"

Lawrence Korb
July 25, 2013

Author's note:

Dr. Korb was Assistant Secretary of Defense (Manpower, Reserve Affairs, Installations, and Logistics) from 1981 to 1985. He currently serves as Senior Fellow at the Center for American Progress, Senior Advisor to the Center for Defense Information, and adjunct professor at Georgetown University. Previously, he has served as a Senior Fellow at the Council on Foreign Relations and the Brookings Institution and Dean of the Graduate School of Public and International Affairs at the University of Pittsburgh.

PREFACE

This book is not intended to be a rigorous academic product or a reference source. In fact, it could be characterized as a very long op-ed piece intended to promote dialogue. It is the product of my thirty-five years of military service, formal military education including the Army War College, study at Harvard's Kennedy School of Government, dialogue with national security experts and soldiers, and ongoing reading and study. The opinions I offer are informed by these experiences. Most of the material presented here (except for that in chapters 2 and 3) is readily available to the general public in their daily newspapers. I have simply pulled this information together to inform this book's central question: Is the all-volunteer force working, and will it work in the future? To address this question, I have focused on the three issues of fairness, efficiency, and sustainability. If we as a society prove unable to respond to this question, we may one day be faced with a far more difficult one: What if we had a war and no one showed up on our side?

ACKNOWLEDGEMENTS

This Project benefitted greatly from the contributions of service members and their families, national security experts, journalists, and academics with whom I have engaged over the past decades. I am particularly indebted to Dr. Andrew Bacevich, Dr. Aaron Belkin, Dr. Nathaniel Frank, Dr. Lawrence Korb, Mark Thompson, MG (Ret.) Gale Pollock, Fred Weed (a decorated Vietnam veteran) and, Jon Ramsdell who read the manuscript and provided valuable feedback. LTC (Ret.) Mike Young and George Knapp, the two best friends a man could have, also provided input and encouragement. And the team of professionals at iuniverse lit the path that all first-time authors must travel.

Matt Austin was my research assistant in the early stages of the project and he was succeeded by Jacob Brandt. The tireless and efficient work of Jacob made the completion of the project possible.

Finally, the counsel of my wife, Colleen, to "stop talking about it and write the book" was invaluable. Her encouragement and tolerance made completion of the book possible and she is delighted by the prospect of my home office being restored to some level of order and tidiness.

All of the assistance acknowledged here has made the book better. Any remaining shortcomings are my responsibility.

CHAPTER 1 – AMERICA AND ITS MILITARY

How the All Volunteer Force widens the gap between the military and the citizens it protects.

In the history of the United States, Americans have embraced a host of laws, policies, practices and value sets that worked toward strengthening our democracy. As time passed, we reevaluated and modified a number of these conventions. These changes occurred not necessarily because the status quo was wrong or misguided but because circumstances changed or because, upon reflection, the people questioned the assumptions or facts that undergirded existing laws, policies, practices, and value sets.

Positive changes that have strengthened American democracy include the elimination of slavery, the achievement of women's suffrage, the repeal of prohibition, expansions of civil rights, Reagan-era tax cuts, and improvements to women's reproductive rights. In the military, changes have included racial integration, gender integration, the all-volunteer force (AVF) and the recent repeal of "Don't Ask, Don't Tell" (DADT). However, not all Americans would agree that all these changes were positive.

None of these changes came easily, and some were particularly troublesome to certain segments of the population. Change is difficult

1

for institutions and even more difficult for individuals acting as change agents, even when maintaining the status quo poses great risk. Indeed, this is particularly true for individual behavior. In their book *Immunity to Change,* Robert Kegan and Lisa Lahey, members of the Change Leadership Group at the Harvard Graduate School of Education, wrote, "not long ago a medical study showed that if heart doctors tell their seriously at risk heart patients that they will literally die if they do not make changes to their personal lives—diet, exercise, smoking—still only one in seven is able to make the change."

Over time, the pace of change has dramatically increased for everyone. This is apparent in America's use of—and increased reliance on—the employment of US armed forces. American service members and their families have endured tremendous hardships and changes that have a number of significant consequences. The United States has been at war since 2001. Some 2.4 million American troops out of a population of 240 million citizens over the age of eighteen have fought in Iraq and Afghanistan—1 percent of the population. This statistic is relevant not only to national military strategy and wartime planning but also to the social fabric of our nation—what has been referred to as civil-military relations. The fact that the AVF makes up such a small percentage of the population was a deliberate manpower consideration from the early planning stages of the Iraq War, as Secretary of Defense Donald Rumsfeld wanted to prove that the "shock and awe" provided by superior technology would be sufficient to ensure victory with minimal troop levels. The Iraq War would be a short affair paid for with Iraqi oil, and the Iraqi people would greet us as liberators. General Eric Shinseki, army chief of staff, assessed it differently and testified before Congress that success in Iraq would require three to four times the number of troops suggested by Rumsfeld and his acolytes. Rumsfeld and Deputy Defense Secretary Paul Wolfowitz publicly pilloried Shinseki immediately after his testimony and pressured him to resign. Later, as the war dragged on, Shinseki's estimates proved correct.

The Iraq War soon morphed into a full-fledged insurgency, if not a civil war. Consequently, the Pentagon faced fighting a long war for the first time since the AVF was implemented in 1973. When a sufficient number of qualified citizens failed to volunteer, the Pentagon reacted with a number of personnel policies geared toward attracting new recruits. For example, the army lowered enlistment standards for high-school graduation, age, and physical fitness. The Pentagon granted the highest number of moral waivers in the history of the AVF, allowing convicted felons and violent criminals to enter its ranks.[1]

As the wars continued, many service members whose terms of enlistment had expired were forced to remain in uniform due to a policy called *stop-loss*. Some critics labeled this a backdoor draft that violated underlying principles of the AVF. The army ignored violations of physical fitness and weight control standards that in peacetime were grounds for discharge. The army paid unprecedented cash bonuses, which were largely tax free, for enlistment and reenlistment. Additionally, the Pentagon employed civilian contractors at an unprecedented level, most notably Halliburton and Blackwater, to execute tasks traditionally performed by uniformed service members. Finally, soldiers and Marines were sent into harm's way for third, fourth, and fifth combat tours, and National Guardsmen and Reservists were sent for second and third tours while 99 percent of their fellow citizens went about their daily lives. Some observers of the Pentagon's personnel policies expressed concern that the army and Marine Corps would break under this strain. Although neither service broke, thousands of service members and their families did as evidenced by unprecedented suicides and divorce rates, post-traumatic stress disorder (PTSD), drug abuse, and veteran homelessness and unemployment. The US government and all Americans will bear the social and financial costs of these tragedies for at least a generation to come. The fact that only 1 percent of the American people were directly involved in these two decade-long wars suggests that a serious gap exists in civil-military relations.

The question of whether such a gap exists is not new. Experts

---

1 See "Army and Marine Corps Grant More Felony Waivers," *New York Times,* Lizette Alverez, April 22, 2008, and "Army Recruiting More Dropouts," *Time Magazine,* Mark Thompson, January 23, 2008.

have expressed a pattern of concern for at least six decades. In 1957, sociologist Samuel Huntington wrote in *The Soldier and the State* that the US military had "the outlook of an estranged minority." In 1986, journalist Arthur Hadley referred to the relationship as "the less than amicable separation of the military from financial, business, political, and intellectual elites of this country, particularly the last two." In 1997, Tom Ricks wrote in the Atlantic that the "American political and economic elite generally don't understand the military" and added, "nor is such an understanding deemed important, even in making national security policy." In fact, the last two chairmen of the House Armed Services Committee, Congressmen Buck Mckeon and Ike Skelton, never served in the military, a situation unprecedented in modern times. Finally, journalist Mark Thompson wrote in a 2012 *Time* cover story that "over the past generation the world's lone superpower has created and grown accustomed to a permanent military caste, increasingly disconnected from US society, waging decade-long wars in its name, no longer representative of or drawn from the citizenry as a whole." What do all of these observations suggest in regard to the health of American civil-military relations today? What is the likelihood—and will the consequence be—of this tug at our social fabric becoming a tear?

This estrangement and consequent deference to the military in general and to the question of how we man our forces in particular may be viewed as a strange twist to the highly publicized Occupy Wall Street movement. The movement characterized itself as a response to the 99 percent being taken advantage of by the 1 percent—that is, the wealthy, powerful, and well connected. The twist is that the 1 percent who serve in our military are similarly being taken advantage of by the 99 percent who do not choose to serve. A moral and ethical element arises in both cases. **Most Americans look at the issue of manning our military through the lens of fear, apathy, ignorance, and guilt—a lens often polished by self-interest and immediate gratification.**

Fear is a powerful force that we often would rather not acknowledge or deal with. We have both collective fears and individual fears, and those fears vary over time depending on the threat and the individual or organization in danger. Collectively, we fear terrorism, a mushroom cloud on the horizon, or the disruption of the flow of oil from the Middle East, to name a few fears that we have come to believe can be dealt with most effectively by our military. Before these fears came to dominance, our nation experienced a series of fears from Barbary pirates to Soviet domination, all of them dealt with by military force. Without fear, the military loses its raison d'être and its budget, prominence, and Beltway influence. Without fear, defense contractors lose billion-dollar weapons contracts. I am not implying that the world is not a dangerous and complex place but that fear drives us to the military-industrial-congressional complex as a convenient savior, and it is more than ready to feed that fear and offer a solution. We may also have a collective, perhaps unconscious, fear of asking ourselves the fundamental question of this book: Is the AVF fair, efficient, and sustainable? Congress may be afraid to entertain a potentially unpopular alternative to the volunteer force and afraid of the political and social pushback it could create. Congress may also fear that an examination of the question of how we man the force will result in a realization that the civil military relationship is broken. That which is unexamined is invisible. Senior members of the military also may fear to entertain this question, as doing so could create difficulties for Congress, upon which the military depends not only for its budget appropriations but also for confirmation of its promotions. The military may also fear that it will be unable to train, lead, and discipline a more representative force that includes nonvolunteers. Volunteers are expected to be compliant. After all, they volunteered.

We also have individual fears, real or imagined, of military service. The surrender of individual rights, the rigors of boot camp, the physical danger of the battlefield, and the long-term physical and mental scars of war make many young Americans who have viable alternatives to military service (and their parents) reluctant to offer their service, and perhaps their lives, to our national security. Parents have even banded together to keep military recruiters from contacting their high-school-aged children and formed a national alliance, Leave My Child Alone![2] The organization offers information on how to protect America's youth against military recruiters. The current volunteer system accommodates these fears.

Second is apathy. Generally, apathy may be a way to deal with fear. If something frightens us, we can deal with the fear by consciously or unconsciously exercising a lack of concern, interest, or emotion. The apathy that we exhibit toward the issue of how we man our military forces or deal with veterans' issues may be part of a wider apathy in our democracy reflected in people's disappointment with the dysfunction in Washington as Congress fails to deal effectively with difficult but important issues. Low voter turnout reflects a collective apathy regarding our democracy. Disparate penalties for white-collar versus street crime and the widening income gap between low wage earners and the wealthy may reflect and fuel apathy. This broad evidence of apathy in our society makes it unsurprising that we might be apathetic toward the issue of how we man our military forces.

We often hear people of good faith saying things like, "It's a shame that he's on his fourth combat tour in Iraq, but he volunteered; who am I to judge his choice?" This is not necessarily a malicious apathy but one born of perceived helplessness and frustration that leads to rationalization and denial. Apathy is reflected in our individual and collective response to the adverse consequences of military service as reflected in veteran homelessness, unemployment, suicide, domestic violence, drug and alcohol abuse, and sexual violence (which the Department of Defense euphemistically labels military sexual trauma). We are even apathetic to our military's conduct, whether it's Blackwater contractors gunning down seventeen innocent civilians in Nissor Square in Iraq or the deaths of innocent civilians that we refer to as collateral damage in drone strikes. At the end of 2012, the Afghan war did not make the Pew Research list of top fifteen news stories or the Associated Press editors and news directors list, and Yahoo's list of top news stories

---

2 LeaveMyChildAlone.org is the organization's website

for 2012 omitted the Afghan war. These omissions existed despite the fact that sixty-eight thousand Americans were fighting—and some of them dying—in Afghanistan at the end of 2012. Michael Dimock, the associate director at the Pew Research Center for People and the Press, said, "the public is having a hard time staying focused on foreign engagements that have been ongoing for over a decade." Those who had skin in the game, though, generally found ways to get the news. A last example of collective apathy is the fact that many of those who have volunteered for military service are now part of a nine-hundred-thousand-case backlog at the Veterans Administration that denies them medical attention for up to two years. As a colleague of mine asks, "Where is the outrage?"

One might like to help but doesn't know where to start, so defers to apathy. A token example is the "Support the Troops" bumper sticker. A more meaningful variation would be a bumper sticker that reads, "Support the Troops ... Enlist." How many Americans have visited seriously injured soldiers and their families at Walter Reed? How many Americans have attended a military funeral in their community? How many Americans have volunteered to help the family of a disabled veteran care for their loved one? Apathy steels us against these uncomfortable realities.

Third is ignorance. Apathy and ignorance go hand in hand. In fact, there's a joke in which a grade-school teacher asks little Johnny, "What's the difference between ignorance and apathy?" Johnny defiantly responds, "I don't know and I don't care." The teacher then says, "Very good, Johnny, very good." I refer to ignorance here not as socially unacceptable behavior but as a lack of knowledge or awareness of a particular thing—in this case national security in general and specifically how we man our military. I realize that most Americans are too engaged in keeping a job (or finding one), paying a mortgage, or funding retirement to take the time to understand geopolitics or military strategy, so they leave these issues to the wisdom of their elected leaders and their appointees and form their opinions based on superficial repetition that reflects and affirms their conservative or liberal biases.

Conservatives watch FOX, and liberals watch MSNBC. After watching, though, few Americans know how many service members have been killed in Iraq and Afghanistan or how many have been seriously injured. Nor do they know the cost of the two wars. We can't even be sure of the mission or our success in Iraq. In 2003, President Bush told us it was accomplished (aboard the USS *Abraham Lincoln*) but the 2012 Army Posture Statement simply says we left Iraq "responsibly"; there is no mention of mission accomplishment or winning. Few are asking if the official assessment of Afghanistan will be any more positive when we depart in 2014.

We find comfort in the idea of American exceptionalism and use it in place of knowledge and rigorous analysis. Often we marginalize those who do not buy into this comforting and dominant view. Dr. Zbigniew Brzezinski, a former national security advisor, writes in his book *Strategic Vision* that a major American "vulnerability is a public that is highly ignorant about the world. The uncomfortable truth is that the US public has an alarmingly limited knowledge of basic global geography, current events, and even pivotal movements in world history."

Finally, we experience guilt. Many Americans, consciously or unconsciously, feel guilt as a result of their choice not to serve in their nation's AVF. The dictionary defines *guilt* as a feeling of culpability, especially for ongoing offenses or from a sense of inadequacy. When lightly challenged, they rationalize or justify their decision and move on. Vice-President Dick Cheney is not considered a dove regarding military issues. Nevertheless, as a young man he secured five deferments from military service during the Vietnam War. When asked why he chose to not serve, he said he had other priorities. As a result of guilt, most Americans are less inclined to question or critique military strategy, call military senior leaders to task, or hold service members rigorously accountable for war crimes or gross deviations from rules of engagement. We are inclined to give American service members the benefit of the doubt, because they are ours and they are doing something for us that we decline to do for ourselves.

We have come to deal with the guilt in subtle ways. One is through the gratuitous use of the word *hero* to refer to all members of the military. According to the formal definition, a hero is an illustrious warrior, a man admired for his achievements and noble qualities, and one that shows great courage. Few service members see themselves as heroes, and most would rather not be referred to as such. But referring to them as heroes reduces the guilt of many. If the 1 percent who serve are heroes, does that imply that the 99 percent who don't are slackers at best or cowards at worst? Some might argue that large nongovernment initiatives like the $50 million Wounded Warrior Program to help seriously wounded Iraq and Afghanistan veterans and their families also serve to soothe guilt and provide the illusion of sacrifice and patriotism for nonveterans. This is a worthy cause that helps veterans, but shouldn't their needs be met by the government that sent them into harm's way rather than charity?

Ninety-nine percent live in the land of the free and the home of the brave because 1 percent who have skin in the game chose to be brave and call that land home. The 99 percent succumb to fear, apathy, ignorance, and guilt to become limited-liability patriots with "Support the Troops" bumper stickers on their cars. They lack the commitment in their minds and hearts that would be required to enlist.

The purpose of this short book is to raise the question of whether the AVF is working and whether it will work into the foreseeable future and at what cost—social, financial, and geopolitical. The question of whether the AVF is working is challenging, because all those who engage the question will likely frame it differently. Differences should be expected based on age, economic class, race, education, occupation, political party, religion, and life experiences. These differences constitute a reality that informs and affects any difficult issue that three hundred million citizens in a free democracy engage. In order to focus the discussion, I use a framework that asks, "Is the AVF fair, efficient, and sustainable?" This is the same framework Dr. Jeffrey D. Sachs uses to examine the American economy in his recent book *The Price of Civilization*.

Fairness suggests that something is marked by impartiality and honesty and free from self-interest, prejudice, and favoritism. Do all citizens participate, contribute, and sacrifice in manning the force, and should they? Is the force representative of our nation in terms of race, gender, class, and region, and should it be? Fairness regarding military service is usually defined in terms of serving or not serving. It could also be defined as all qualified citizens between the ages of eighteen and twenty-four being subjected to enlistment based on a transparent random selection process. The fairness question has historically been framed by the philosophical tension between libertarianism and egalitarianism. Libertarianism holds that an individual has no responsibility to society or the state other than to respect the liberty and property of others; the individual, according to this philosophy, has absolute, unrestricted liberty of thought and action. Egalitarianism, on the other hand, is a belief in human equality with respect to social, political, and economic rights, privileges, and responsibilities and advocates the removal of inequalities among people. Dr. Elliot Cohen writes in *Citizens and Soldiers,* "we may sum this up crudely by saying that liberals hope to minimize coercion and egalitarians to spread it evenly."

Efficiency suggests that the method of manning the force produces the desired effect without waste and redundancy at a reasonable cost. Does the US military efficiently "provide for the common defense" in fighting and winning America's wars? If so, at what cost and to whom? The Center for Strategic and Budgetary Assessment has reported that "Over the past decade, the cost per person in the active duty force increased by 46 percent. If personnel costs continue to grow at that rate and the overall defense budget remains flat with inflation, military personnel costs will consume the entire defense budget by 2039." Both budget cost and opportunity cost must be considered. Treasure is a critical measure of cost, but so are blood, personal sacrifice, and the individual long-term scars of war.

Sustainability denotes the capacity of the system to maintain current or expected results over a period appropriate to its mission. In this case, is the volunteer system capable of providing the required quantity and quality of manpower for military service today and into the future? In a January 2013 report to the secretary of defense, the Reserve Forces

Policy Board stated that "The fully burdened and life cycle cost trends supporting the current All-Volunteer Force are unsustainable."

Engaging the fair, efficient, and sustainable criteria facilitates structured thought and dialogue in answering the critical question, Is the AVF working, and will it work in the future?

This book is intended to be descriptive rather than prescriptive. Since 1973, when the AVF was instituted, the world has changed dramatically. Globalization became the driver of our economy, the Cold War ended, the Soviet Union crumbled, the Internet was born, the United States became a large debtor nation, terrorism emerged as a threat, the baby boom passed, and adolescent obesity and a 25 percent high-school dropout rate became national concerns. Even assuming that the move to the AVF was the best method for America to man its military forces to support national security in 1973, is it reasonable to assume (given all that has changed since 1973) that it is still the best method today and into the future? Only a civil, fact-based dialogue among concerned and informed Americans, all of whom have skin in the game, can answer this critical question.

CHAPTER 2 – A HISTORY OF MANNING THE FORCE

Conscription "worked" for two centuries; conscripted militaries won the Revolutionary War, the Civil War, WWI and WWII.

As with most complex and sometimes contentious policy issues, such as how a nation mans its military forces, a little history and the context it provides is helpful. History helps us know how we got to where we are and where we might go in the future. Philosopher George Santayana said, "Those who do not remember the past are condemned to repeat it." Throughout history, nations have taken different approaches to manning their militaries dating back to the Romans. For the purposes of this book, I will restrict the history review to the United States going back to the Civil War—the first time that force manning became a critical issue in the United States.

Before exploring the Civil War experience and beyond, one short digression seems appropriate. There is much discussion today about our founding fathers and their intentions. **General George Washington, perhaps the most respected of those founding fathers, said in 1783, "it may be laid down as a primary position, and the basis of our system,**

that every citizen who enjoys the protection of a free government, owes not only a portion of his property, but even of his personal services to the defense of it." [3] This principle led President Washington, in 1792, to sign the Uniform Militia Act, which stipulated that "each and every free able bodied white male citizen of the respective States, resident therein, who is or shall be of age eighteen years, and under age of forty-five years ... shall severally and respectively be enrolled in the militia." The militia is, of course, the predecessor of today's National Guard. At the other end of the timeline and the philosophical spectrum was the 1969 Gates Commission appointed by President Nixon, which stated, "we unanimously believe that the nation's interests will be better served by an all volunteer force ... and it will strengthen our freedoms. This minimizes government interference with the freedom of the individual." The report further stated that the draft has "weakened the political fabric of our society and impaired the delicate web of shared values that alone enable a free society to exist." The history of the time separating these two diametrically opposed ways of manning our military follows.

The Civil War

Although recruiting in the US Army dates back to 1775 in order to fill the ranks to fight the Revolutionary War, it was not until 1822 that the army's General Recruiting Service was established. The states raised militias using a quota system and, in times of crisis, manpower raised by the states was integrated and placed into federal service. Article I of the Constitution gave Congress the power "to raise and support Armies" and "to provide for calling forth the Militia to execute the Laws of the Union, suppress insurrections, and repel invasions." The debate that led to this article of the Constitution was interesting in that it was not focused on compulsory service verses volunteerism but on standing armies verses citizen-militia armies. The founding fathers were influenced by their experience with Britain's standing army. The

---

3 "The Evolution of the All-Volunteer Force", Bernard Rostker, RAND Corp., Santa Monica, CA, 2006, p.20.

constitution did not specifically state that conscription was within the power of the new government. Until the Civil War, the militia quota system (with some minor variations) remained the method by which America manned its military forces.

The reality and manpower requirements of the Civil War changed everything. This was the first time that the United States was required to mobilize the entire population to achieve its strategic objective, which was to reunite the seceded South with the North. Hundreds of thousands of troops were required to fight across a thousand-mile front and defend critical assets. After an initial rush of volunteers, both sides quickly realized that the old militia quota and volunteer system was inadequate. Conscription was the only answer.

The South was first to move to conscription. By a strong majority, the Confederate Congress enacted a conscription law on April 16, 1862. The law provided that all white males between the ages of eighteen and thirty-five were subject to conscription in the Confederate army for up to three years. As the war proceeded, these age limits were expanded to seventeen and fifty, reflecting mounting battle casualties and a smaller population from which to draw. Despite the strong legislative support of these conscription laws, the draft was able to produce only about one-third of the Confederacy's manpower requirements, as other officials created policies and means by which certain groups and classes were exempted from conscription. Thus, the first conscription laws were followed closely by the first efforts for deferment and exemption.

The North followed closely behind the South in dealing with its manpower shortfalls. The Militia Act of 1862 gave President Lincoln the authority to draft manpower from states that failed to meet their quota of volunteers. President Lincoln never had to exercise this authority, as the threat of conscription laid out in the Militia Act caused an increase in volunteers sufficient to meet the Union army's manpower needs in the early stages of the war—an important data point related to the effect of conscription on volunteerism. Casualties and the broadening scope of the war forced the North to take additional steps to man its force. Congress passed the Enrollment Act of 1863 on March 3 under Article I of the Constitution, which gave Congress the authority "to raise and support armies." All male citizens between the ages of twenty and forty-five were subject to military service for three years or until the end of the war, whichever occurred first. The law included a provision for substitution and commutation, allowing a draftee to purchase exemption for $300.

This substitution and commutation provision presented a problem in 1863 and presents a different problem today. In 1863, the problem was real. Author David Nasaw writes that Andrew Carnegie, the billionaire rail and steel baron, upon receiving his draft notice, paid an Irish immigrant to report in his place. He was not alone in his actions as a perfectly legal draft dodger. In fact, Nasaw writes, "A large number of men of his generation, who would later be referred to as 'robber barons' including Phillip Armour, Jay Cooke, J.P. Morgan, George Pullman, Jay Gould, Jim Fisk, Collis P. Huntington, and John D. Rockefeller spent the war as he did, making money by providing the Union Armies with fuel, uniforms, shoes, rifles, ammunition, provisions, transportation, and financing." Since only wealthy citizens from an elite upper socioeconomic class were able to afford such a fee, the burden of fighting and dying fell disproportionately on poor and working-class citizens, generating the slogan, "A rich man's war and a poor man's fight." Slogans morphed into violence as thousands of irate citizens took to the streets in the 1863 New York Draft Riots in protest. As many as two thousand protesters were killed and eight thousand injured. Many people argued at the time that the umbrage taken by the rioters was clearly understandable and probably justified. Most Americans, when they learn about the commutation and substitution provision of the 1863 law, are surprised and disappointed that such a clearly undemocratic policy could have existed at a time when the very existence of our nation was at stake. This leads to today's problem.

Although today most Americans would agree that the Civil War commutation and substitution provisions were undemocratic at best and deplorable at worst, we are doing effectively the same thing today in our recruiting practices, albeit under the cover of collective approval.

In 2007, 70 percent of those inducted into the US Army received enlistment bonuses. The bonuses averaged $18,000. If one assumes an inflation rate of 3 percent from 1862 to 2007, $18,000 today is roughly equivalent to $300 during the Civil War. The only difference is that the enlistment bonus is paid by taxpayer dollars, while Carnegie paid the $300 himself. In both cases financial inducements were more attractive to the lower socioeconomic classes than the upper classes, thus relieving the upper classes of the risk and sacrifices of military service.

The draft law encouraged many to enlist in order to avoid conscription; these recruits were the first draft-induced volunteers. The North inducted more than 2.6 million men into the service, but only 6% were conscripted. The states paid sizable bounties to meet their quotas, and the Civil War was the last conflict until the 1991 Gulf War in which the United States relied on the system of volunteers and the organized militia to fill its wartime ranks. Technically, it was also the last time that commutation and substitution would be allowed.

World War I

America filled its military ranks to fight World War I influenced by politics, the lessons of the Civil War, activists in the War Department, and interest groups like the Army League, the National Security League, and the National Association for Universal Military Training. All of these players inside and outside the government supported conscription as opposed to volunteerism. Minimal opposition to the draft existed, and draft dodgers were dealt with harshly.

The political aspect centered on President Woodrow Wilson, who advocated for the United States to distance itself from the European war. However, in his State of the Union message to Congress on December 8, 1914, Wilson stated that he believed that if we entered the war manning requirements could be met via volunteers without any need for conscription. The assembled lawmakers cheered his comments. Nonetheless, Congress passed the Selective Service Act of 1917 by a wide margin. Politically, President Wilson came to view conscription as a fair and efficient means of raising manpower, drawing on the lessons of both Union and Confederate problems in the Civil War. Specifically, the decision was informed by the post–Civil War recommendation of Brigadier General James Oaks that "it be the citizen's responsibility to register in future drafts; that substitution, commutation, and bounties be rejected forever; and that the central government take over full responsibility for the draft rather than depend on the states for help."

A second political influence on Wilson's decision was former president Theodore Roosevelt. Roosevelt was one of the leading critics of Wilson on a number of issues. He proposed to raise a volunteer division and lead it into France, the effect of which would have been to upstage Wilson at a time when he (and in his view the nation) could least afford it. Conscription would blunt Roosevelt's effort and his threat to Wilson.

Despite the unambiguous position expressed in Wilson's 1914 State of the Union address, much of the activity in his War Department in the two years that followed focused on conscription. Secretary of War Newton Baker and General Hugh L. Scott, army chief of staff, felt strongly that conscription was preferable to a reliance on volunteerism. They played leading roles in pushing legislation supporting conscription through Congress. In 1916, General Scott testified before the House Military Affairs Committee that he favored conscription, knowing that his testimony did not conform to the President's position. He couched his testimony by noting, "I speak only for myself." Scott's testimony is reminiscent of that of General Eric Shinseki advocating for a larger force to invade Iraq, contrary to his superiors' positions. The difference is that Scott's advice was taken; Shinseki's was not.

Scott went on to have comprehensive studies conducted within the War Department that dealt with selection processes, training systems and facilities, and logistics issues. These studies laid the strategic and operational foundation for America to move to a war footing efficiently. The product of these studies was the National Army Plan, which General Scott approved on February 14, 1917. An indication of the rigor and comprehensive nature of the plan is that Secretary Baker submitted it to Congress just nine days later. After heated debate that lasted more than a month, the legislation authorizing conscription passed by solid majorities on May 18, 1917. Passage of the legislation was aided by the previously mentioned interest groups and the Plattsburg movement led by Major General Leonard Wood, which was a voluntary military training program attended by many prominent business and professional leaders.

The draft was largely seen as fair and effective, given the application of lessons learned in the Civil War draft. The act established a "liability for military service of all male citizens" between the ages of twenty-one and thirty-one (later eighteen and forty-five); prohibited bounties, substitutions, and commutations; allowed exemptions only for dependency, essential occupations, and religious considerations, and was administered by local boards composed of leading civilians in each community. Draft calls and deferments were issued by those local boards based on an order of numbers drawn in a national lottery. The draft proceeded with little opposition, as 24 million men were registered in 1917–1918 and almost 3 million were inducted.

Although the World War I draft process was both efficient and effective, it was not completely free of criticism and opposition. Perhaps because of the perceived fairness of the World War I draft process and a sense that the nation was in jeopardy, those who refused to comply were dealt with rather harshly. Those who refused induction were often sentenced to twenty-year prison terms. In 1918, Secretary of War Baker sent the Board of Inquiry to deal with claims of conscientious objection. The tribunals found many to be frauds and sentenced 345 to penal labor camps, 142 to life imprisonment, and, notably, 17 to death. Most of those convicted were pardoned after the war and received dishonorable discharges. Eugene Debs, a prominent union leader, was also imprisoned for "obstructing the recruitment or enlistment service" and ran for president in 1920 from his Atlanta prison cell. He was subsequently pardoned by President Harding.

The most significant opposition came in 1917 when a coalition of draft opponents led by Emma Goldman challenged the new draft law in federal court on the grounds that it violated the Thirteenth Amendment, which prohibited slavery and involuntary servitude. The suit worked its way to the Supreme Court, which unanimously upheld the constitutionality of the 1917 Draft Law, noting that Congress has the power to declare war and to raise and support armies. **The court's decision specifically stated that "it may not be doubted that the very conception of a just government and its duty to the citizen includes the reciprocal obligation of the citizen to render military service in case of need, and the right to compel it." The court's decision stands to this day.**

The draft ended in 1918, but the military saw a need to continue to plan for future wars through conscription. In 1926, the army established a Joint Army-Navy Selective Service Committee. The committee did not receive congressional approval and funding until 1934, when Major Lewis Hershey was assigned to the committee. Hershey and others worked diligently to develop a selective service system, which Hershey would head for almost forty years. Their work was reflected in the Selective Service and Training Act of 1940.

World War II

In 1940, as Germany took over France, the US government had done little to prepare the nation to meet its potential manpower requirements if it had to enter the war. President Roosevelt was concerned that the implementation of a peacetime draft would be a political liability in an election year. This concern was eliminated as his Republican opponent, Wendell Willkie, proposed selective conscription as war clouds gathered. Granville Clark, an influential attorney who led the National Emergency Committee of the Military Training Corps Association, also urged conscription. The committee played a key role in writing and securing the passage of the Selective Service and Training Act (STSA) of 1940 by mobilizing America's upper classes in support of passage. Americans overwhelmingly supported conscription, as they felt threatened by the German-Italian alliance after the Japanese attack on Pearl Harbor. Roosevelt and the War Department did not lead on the issue of conscription.

The STSA, America's first peacetime draft, became law on September 16, 1940. It was largely modeled after the World War I draft process and was generally well received and judged to be fair. Nearly 50 million men registered, and 10 million were inducted. The draft provided nearly two-thirds of the nation's manpower requirements, enabling the military to reach its peak of 8.3 million men in 1945. Initially, men between the ages of twenty-one and forty-five were subject to one year's service based on a national lottery. The term of service was expanded to two years in August 1941 and, after Pearl Harbor, extended again to the duration of the war plus six months. At the same time, the law was changed to require the registration of all men up to the age of sixty-four. Reality prevailed over the initial plans.

There was limited opposition to the draft in World War II, and it came principally from African Americans in the North. Muslims and communists dropped their opposition when Germany attacked Russia in 1941. There were no substantive legal challenges as there had been in 1917. There were conscientious objectors, 72 percent of whom were granted CO status. Most of them were required to serve in noncombat roles, and six thousand were imprisoned. With the nation so supportive of the war, conscientious objectors and draft dodgers were dealt with sternly by the courts.

The Cold War

With the end of World War II, many military leaders, elected officials, and the general public believed that the need for conscription had ended even though STSA was extended until March 31, 1947. Two realities then converged to make government officials rethink the question. First, the army was securing less than half of its required enlistees per month without the threat of conscription and was one hundred thousand soldiers under strength. The army has historically experienced the greatest recruiting difficulties among the services. Second, the Soviet

Union was emerging as a global threat to US interests. In response, Congress passed the Selective Service Act of 1948 requiring that all males aged eighteen to twenty-six register and be subject to twenty-one months of active federal service. The military ranks were quickly filled by conscripts and volunteers motivated by the threat of conscription who wished to have some choice of assignment.

The beginning of the Korean War in June of 1950 validated the wisdom of those who advocated for the Selective Service Act of 1948. Without it, the United States would have been even more unprepared for the conflict. The act was extended and modified as the Universal Military Training and Service Act of 1951, which expanded the president's authority to extend terms of service to four years, lowered the draft age to eighteen, and canceled deferments for married men without children.

Even after the end of the Korean War in 1953, the draft was continued throughout the 1950s and 1960s despite periodic objections to its continuation. From a geopolitical standpoint, the draft demonstrated American resolve to the Soviet threat and supported an alternative to the Mutually Assured Destruction doctrine of the two superpowers. The Reserve Forces Act of 1955 was intended to help man the force and improve the readiness of the reserve components as well as to constrain the military's employment by the president. In addition to demonstrating national resolve, there were several arguments supporting continued conscription that are relevant to current analysis. The draft stimulated overall enlistment, especially among higher aptitude candidates; the threat of conscription stimulated Reserve Officer Training Corps (ROTC) enrollment; and the draft supported reserve-component enlistments. The absence of a draft in 1947–1948 led to serious shortfalls in enlistments. Vietnam and its social and political ramifications changed the course of conscription in the United States for decades.

The Vietnam War

American presidents were sensitive to political and social effects of conscription even before and during the very early stages of the

Vietnam War. Before President Kennedy executed his decision to send military advisors to Vietnam, he directed the Selective Service Director Lewis Hershey (off the record) to draft married men with children last and married men next to last. When President Johnson, in 1965, considered sending significant numbers of reinforcements to Vietnam, he considered sending draftees or volunteers or calling up reserve units. Despite President Eisenhower's counsel not to send draftees, as it would cause a "major public relations problem," he did so anyway. Little did either know how correct Eisenhower's assessment would prove to be.

There was opposition to the draft even before major US involvement in Vietnam began as large numbers of baby boomers became eligible for the draft, driving a large number of deferments for college and graduate students, who enjoyed preferred postings even if drafted. High-school dropouts were twice as likely to be drafted as college graduates, renewing cries from the Civil War; once again it was a rich man's war and a poor man's fight. Historian Robert Griffith notes that "inductions from 1954 to 1964 averaged 100,000 per year. As American involvement in Vietnam escalated, so did conscription. In 1966, 400,000 were called. Casualties also increased, especially among draftees. Draftees, who constituted only 16 percent of the armed forces, but 88 percent of infantry solders in Vietnam, accounted for over 50 percent of the combat deaths in 1969, a peak year for casualties. Little wonder that the draft became the focus of anti-Vietnam activism."

The Veteran's Administration has reported that between 1964 and 1975, 9.2 million men served in the military, 3.5 million in Vietnam, out of a national pool of 27 million. During this period, approximately 2.2 million were drafted, and several times as many were draft-induced volunteers, many of whom sought to avoid combat by having some control over their assignments. As the war dragged on, draft opposition became widespread and, in some cases, violent. Draft avoidance and evasion became rampant. As many as one hundred thousand draft-eligible men fled the country to avoid induction. The draft, perceived by most to be unfairly executed by an unpopular president, became a victim of the most unpopular war in American history. One may speculate as to whether a draft without exemption and deferments or the broader employment of the National Guard and reserve forces in Vietnam might have changed America's view of conscription. The reality is that political and social forces drove national leaders to seek an alternative method to man the force.

In summary, these draft periods show various similarities and differences. Most people believe that Congress plays the dominant role in manning the force because of its constitutional mandate to raise and support armies. But each period offered different leaders. The Civil War had President Lincoln and Secretary of War Stanton playing a key behind-the-scenes role in Congressional actions. In World War I, the principal actor was the military, led by the army general staff at the direction of General Scott in urging President Wilson to pursue conscription. In World War II, a private citizen named Greenville Clark and other groups outside the government pressured Congress to consider conscription despite the fact that both President Roosevelt and the military were slow to react to a looming threat. During the Cold War, the president was again the dominant actor and remained so through the creation of the AVF. The dominant similarity is that in each period when the threat became apparent and volunteerism fell short, the nation turned to conscription. Winston Churchill said, "you can always count on Americans to do the right thing—after they've tried everything else."

In addition to comparing the dominant players in these periods, one must compare their level of acceptance by the American people. The Civil War draft experienced significant resistance centered on the policies of commutation and substitution, which were widely perceived to be unfair and discriminatory and impacted efficiency due to high desertion rates. The drafts during World War I, World War II, and the early period of the Cold War (1947–1963) were largely perceived to be fair and efficient, as there were no provisions for commutation and substitution, and local draft boards granted deferments parsimoniously. The sustainability of drafts during these periods was also strengthened by the sense that these wars were fought to defend genuine vital national interests. During the Vietnam period, the draft lost broad support not only because it supported a long, unpopular war but also because it came to be viewed as unfair to the lower classes and minorities and favored the upper class through deferments. The fact that a disproportionate number of minorities were assigned to infantry units and experienced high casualty rates also contributed to the negative view of the Vietnam-period draft. The perceived lack of fairness led to reduced efficiency and sustainability.

CHAPTER 3 – NIXON AND THE GATES COMMISSION

When politics trumps national security. Conscription sacrificed at the alter of the most unpopular war in U.S. history.

Richard Nixon campaigned for president leading up to the 1968 election on a platform that included ending the draft. Whether this was an opportunistic position assumed by a politician who was later disgraced or an enlightened initiative adopted by a leader to heal the wounds of a divided nation is still open to debate. The fact is that Nixon saw ending the draft as a means to undermine the anti–Vietnam War movement, secure draft-age voters to his side, and win support from the American academic and liberal sectors. Conscription may have been tried and convicted in a court of politics, popular opinion, and economics by a jury that excluded rigorous consideration of national security. The one notable exception to the national security void in the decision surrounding the AVF is the link between the draft, an unpopular war, and US grand strategy. Andrew Bacevich in his 2010 book *Washington Rules* notes that "with a strategy of global presence, power projection, and interventionism no longer guaranteeing success, alternative approaches to national security strategy might even gain a hearing at home, with this basic strategy no longer taken as given. To those whose interests were served by preserving that strategy, this was an intolerable prospect. So among the explanations for the Vietnam war we can add this one: It was fought to sustain the Washington consensus." Avoiding the "hearing at home" was possible largely because of fear, apathy, ignorance, and guilt. To a degree, all contributed to a national failure to ask first-order, fundamental questions as a result of the outcome in Vietnam. The end of conscription was thus used to discourage genuine inquiry.

Concerns over conscription were evident within the Pentagon and Congress long before the largest draft calls and greatest public protest surfaced. In 1964, Secretary of Defense Robert McNamara commissioned a study headed by William Gorham, a deputy assistant secretary of defense, to "estimate the budgeting cost of shifting from the draft to a volunteer system of manpower procurement." Gorham recruited Dr. Walter Oi of the University of Washington to head the Economic Analysis Division for the study. Dr. Oi would go on to be a central figure in the debate regarding the AVF for decades, advancing the argument that the true cost of the draft was an economic cost rather than simply a budgeting cost because of the hidden tax penalty paid by the draftees. The study recommended ending the draft based on economic assumptions that the incremental budget increase would be between $4 and $17 billion per year but more importantly assumed that force levels could be reduced to those reached prior to the Korean War. The latter assumption was made in the face of rising draft calls to support the Vietnam War. Economics and reality collided; reality won.

The release of the study prompted further action regarding selective service by both President Johnson and Congress in 1966 as opposition to the Vietnam War was steadily growing. President Johnson created the Presidential Advisory Commission on Selective Service headed by Burke Marshall, then general counsel of IBM. Some viewed the commission as an effort by the president to sidestep Congress. Congress set up its own group in the form of a civilian advisory panel headed by retired

US Army General Mark Clark. Both panels dealt with two issues: 1) whether the nation should move to an AVF force and 2) whether the draft should be reformed and, if so, how. Both groups recommended against moving to an all-volunteer force, presumably because the cost was deemed unbearable. Academics were represented in both groups. Prominent figures outside these groups also weighed in against an all-volunteer force. Anthropologist Margaret Mead advocated for a universal national service system as a bridge from adolescence to adulthood. Morris Janowitz, the leading military sociologist of the time, argued that the all-volunteer enlisted force would be predominantly or all African American and a threat to democracy. **Finally, Dr. Henry A. Marmion, president of St. Xavior College, argued "in point of fact, an all volunteer army would liberate the middle class from the legal necessity of serving but commit others to compulsory service by economic circumstances. Is this not, in effect, forcing the poor and the less fortunate into the armed forces? Is this truly democratic?"[4]**

The groups differed, however, regarding reforming the draft. The Marshall Commission recommended that most educational and occupational deferments be eliminated because they were unfair, that the youngest rather than the oldest be called first in order to facilitate career planning, that a national lottery be established, and that local boards be consolidated. The Clark panel disagreed with the commission's position regarding deferments and the lottery. It is interesting to speculate how the course of the Vietnam War and the conscription issue might have changed had all of the Burke Commission recommendations been implemented in 1966.

President Johnson, faced with a widening war and two sets of recommendations from highly respected groups, formed a third group to resolve the tension and provide political cover. He directed the secretary of defense, the director of the Selective Service System, and the director of the Bureau of Budget to establish a joint task force to review

---

4 "The Case Against a Volunteer Army: Should America's Wars Be Fought Only By the Poor and the Black?", Chicago, Quadrangle Books, 1971, p. 46.

the recommendations for reform of the Selective Service System. None of these principals had any institutional motivation for recommending change, and all had a vested interest in the status quo. To no one's surprise, the task force recommended that no changes be made. Four costly years later, some of the Marshall Commission recommendations were implemented.

The recommendations of those three panels led some in Congress to call for an all-volunteer force and framed some debate. But in passing the Military Selective Service Act of 1967, Congress rejected the idea of an all-volunteer force. More importantly, the act prevented the president from implementing a lottery to draft younger men first and protected undergraduate deferments. The tyranny of the status quo overpowered critical analysis and timely action. Gus Lee and Geoffery Parker wrote in *Ending the Draft: The Story of the All Volunteer Force* that "the failure of Congress and the Johnson Administration to reform the draft in 1967 was important to the evolution of the All Volunteer Force. That failure, combined with high draft calls, and increased opposition to the war and the draft assured that the draft would be a major issue during the 1968 presidential campaign. In October of that year, the Republican candidate for president, Richard Nixon, declared his intention to move toward ending the draft when the war in Vietnam was over."

Nixon's political instincts were supported, if not prodded, by the work of Martin Anderson, an associate professor of business at Columbia University. Anderson was a conservative policy expert who challenged a number of liberal programs and took on the draft principally from an economic perspective. He argued that unreasonably low pay for new enlistees made the draft necessary and higher pay would prod volunteers, raise the quality of enlistees, and enhance fairness in manning the force. Several papers Anderson wrote for Nixon were widely circulated among Nixon's advisors. Anderson would become a guiding intellectual advocate for the move toward the AVF and its implementation for decades. His approach to the question of the draft as an economic issue was supported by several other prominent economists and economic forums. Economists emerged as activists on the issue and invaded the arena of sociologists, psychologists, and psychometricians who were interested in testing, classifying, and assigning new recruits. The economists were interested in the higher order issue of how the recruits were secured. In 1966, prominent sociologists Morris Janowitz and Charles Moskos argued against an AVF based on concern over the relationship between the military and the public (the civil-military relationship) and reduced military effectiveness. Defense Secretary Robert McNamara, who valued hard data and systems analysis, welcomed the emergence of an economic framework for the manpower issue. The assignment of William Gorham, an economist, as deputy secretary of defense and his assignment to head the 1964 Pentagon Draft Study further advanced an economic approach.

The economists brought to the discussion the concept of economic costs, a concept advocated most forcefully by Milton Friedman. Friedman stated that when a draftee is "forced to serve, we are in effect imposing on him a tax in kind equal in value to the difference between what it would take to attract him and the military pay he actually receives. This implicit tax in kind should be added to the explicit taxes imposed on the rest of us to get the real cost of our armed forces." The executive branch of government, including the Pentagon, and Congress viewed the issue as a budget cost that did not include the implicit tax. Friedman's argument opened a new area for economists that would culminate in economic analysis dominating the deliberations and recommendations of the Gates Commission in 1973.

Although a number of high-level studies were conducted during this period by noted economists, a study done in 1974 sheds light on the inequalities during the Vietnam period that drove public sentiment and government policy. In their book *Chance and Circumstance: The Draft, the War, and the Vietnam Generation* based on their work on President Ford's Presidential Clemency Board, Lawrence Baker and William Strauss classified service by income and educational status. They identified 26.8 million draft-eligible men in the Vietnam generation, of which 8.7 million enlisted and 2.2 million were drafted. Although most never served in Vietnam in combat or noncombat roles, the following table from their study clearly shows inequality of risk related to both income and education, with income being most influential, reflecting the Civil War cry of "a rich man's war and a poor man's fight."

Likelihood of Vietnam era service (%)

	Military Service	Vietnam Service	Combat Service
Income			
Low	40	19	15
Middle	30	12	7
High	24	9	7
Education			
High-School Dropout	42	18	14
High-School Graduate	45	21	17
College Graduate	23	12	9

Clearly, college graduates from high-income backgrounds fared better than high-school dropouts from low-income backgrounds in avoiding the risks of war in this period.

With Richard Nixon's election as president on November 5, 1968, his transition team moved to prioritize and act on issues to be addressed by the new administration. Arthur Burns and Martin Anderson, both economists with shared roots at Columbia University, were part of the transition team with Anderson having been involved previously in the conscription and selective service issues. Burns immediately engaged William Meckling, dean of the Graduate School of Management at the University of Rochester, who assembled a team to research and develop a recommendation to end conscription. The plan was generated in less than two weeks and prompted Burns to advocate for the formation of a special presidential commission to deal with AVF issues. At a National Security Council meeting in the first week of the new administration, President Nixon raised the issue of the AVF and reforming selective service. The administration saw the two issues as important and closely related but requiring different strategies and timelines; Nixon asked Secretary of Defense Melvin Laird for separate position papers on the issues. Laird's days of leading on these issues and controlling events were numbered.

Shortly after the National Security Council meeting, Nixon directed Laird to plan for a special commission whose purpose was to develop a detailed plan for ending conscription. While Laird favored an AVF, he was not in favor of a special commission so early in the administration and before he had the opportunity to do preparatory work within the Department of Defense (DOD). In his reply to Nixon, he expressed reservations to the commission and identified that steps were already underway at the Pentagon to move toward the AVF; Laird was referring to Project Volunteer.

Project Volunteer had begun the previous fall at the suggestion of the chairman of the House Armed Services Committee, Mendel L. Rivers. The purpose of the project was to study economic and manpower issues in order to maximize the number of men volunteering for military service. Laird attempted to slow Nixon's move toward a special commission using Project Volunteer as an alternative, but Nixon's senior staff interpreted Laird's response as foot-dragging and an insufficient response to the president's intent. Nixon, on the recommendation of Burns and other senior staff, informed Laird that he would proceed with the special commission and that Laird was to continue the work on Project Volunteer, which Nixon applauded. He also told Laird the special commission would integrate Pentagon experts and Laird would have the opportunity to review the commission work in draft and make recommendations. Finally, he asked Laird to recommend members for the special commission. The first name on Laird's list was former Secretary of Defense Thomas Gates. **Nixon's charge to the commission was "to develop a comprehensive plan for eliminating conscription**

and moving toward an all volunteer armed force."[5] Nixon was crystal clear as to what he expected from the commission.

The ultimate recommendation of the Gates Commission was predictable based on President Nixon's position during the campaign, the fact that elimination of the draft was part of the Republican Party platform, and Nixon's charge to the commission noted above. The outcome was further ensured by the composition of the commission and the research staff selected to support it. Although the commission was nominally headed by Secretary Gates, who initially expressed some reservations regarding the AVF, the intellectual strength of the commission rested with outspoken advocates of the AVF and included Milton Friedman, Alan Greenspan, H. Allen Wallis, and Stephan Herbrits. The research staff, which included Walter Oi and Stuart Setman, was dominated by individuals who came from the group at the University of Rochester that had prepared the earlier study for Arthur Burns and participated in the 1964 Pentagon Draft Study.

At the same time that the Gates Commission was forming and beginning its work, Secretary of Defense Laird began his work on reforming the draft, knowing that its elimination was the long-term goal. The centerpiece of Laird's recommendation was that the draft call should be executed by lottery, which would require congressional approval, and that the draft call should be focused on nineteen-year-olds, whose draft liability would be terminated upon reaching age twenty if they were not called, except in emergencies. Congress did not act on the draft reform legislation until November 1969. The legislation gave President Nixon the opportunity to remove some inequalities of the draft consistent with Laird's recommendations.

Although some members of Congress had reservations about or outright disagreed with the draft reform legislation, the strongest objections to the reforms came from the director of Selective Service, General Lewis Hershey, who had lead the Selective Service since 1940.

---

[5] "Statement by the President Announcing a Commission on an All-Volunteer Armed Forces", Washington, D.C.; office of the White House Press Secretary, March 27, 1969

Hershey believed that the system was working well and there was no need for change. The White House believed that not only the system but also its leader, General Hershey, was in need of change. A year-long behind-the-scenes bureaucratic battle ended with General Hershey being removed as head of the Selective Service on February 16, 1970. During this period, he fought against every reform sought by the administration and continued to do so from his new position as manpower mobilization advisor to the president. He went so far as to tell the president, in writing, that the reforms the administration was implementing—specifically a national sequence call, restricting student deferments, and the uniform processing of those drafted—were a perversion of the intent of Congress. His objection fell on deaf ears, and after 1970 he was a nonplayer on manpower mobilization issues. President Nixon was forced to withdraw the nomination of his first choice to replace General Hershey, Charles Dibane, due to opposition in the Senate. His second nominee, Curtis Tarr, was unanimously approved by the Senate Armed Services Committee.

The first meeting of the Gates Commission was held on May 15, 1969, at the White House, and President Nixon participated in a portion of the meeting. Chairman Gates stated that members were not required to recommend a move to an all-volunteer force, notwithstanding Nixon's charge to the commission and the public opinions expressed by some members and some of the support staff. Some initial reservations were expressed at the first meeting, as noted by Gus Lee and Geoffrey Parker in their 1977 book *Ending of the Draft*. Chairman Gates expressed concerns that the hidden tax argument would be difficult to explain to Congress and the public. "Mr. Greenwalt thought that the burden of combat in a volunteer force would fall upon the 'poor and the black' and that there was something immoral about seducing them to die for their country with offers of higher pay. General Norstad ... felt that elimination of the draft could mean that people with better education and backgrounds would not enlist and that the military services would be less effective as a result. It is interesting to note that the commission did all its work behind closed doors and did not hold public hearings despite the fact that the issue with which they dealt had significant public policy, political, and national security implications. In just six months, in December 1969, the commission reached a unanimous agreement that the nation should move to an all-volunteer force—a recommendation that surprised no one given the president's mandate to the commission.

Although the commission recommended movement to the AVF, there were two issues of concern that they left unanswered. The first was the issue of medical professionals and whether a sufficient number could be recruited as true volunteers. The commission recommended that the military contract out as much of the medical care requirement of the DOD as possible, that compensation for medical professionals be increased to attract more to enlist, and that scholarships for medical education be increased with a requirement for service upon graduation. A second area of concern was the reserve components. The members of the commission strongly believed that a significant portion of those serving in the reserve components were doing so to avoid being drafted into the active forces. In response, the commission recommended that the number of reserve-component authorized personnel be reduced by 113,000 and that compensation for first-term enlistees be significantly increased. They also recommended that the reserve components recruit more service members leaving active service and that the reserve components significantly improve their abysmally low retention notes. The commission made no recommendation as to how the reserve components might accomplish these two difficult tasks. There was not a high level of confidence that these two problem areas could be readily resolved by the recommended measures.

As the commission moved to complete its work in late 1969 and began the interagency coordination process, it became clear that the DOD and the army in particular had major disagreements with the recommendations of the commission. The principal differences centered on the cost estimates to implement the AVF and the commission view that increased compensation was the best means to implement the AVF. The army felt that improved personnel policies represented the best method to implement the AVF. These objections were but two of many expressed to or anticipated by the commission.

The commission anticipated other objections to its recommendations and went so far as to include nine specific objections and a rebuttal to each in their report, just as any marketing plan or sales presentation would. The application of marketing principles to national security was a bit unusual. The objections identified by the commission and the commission's rebuttals follow. I have added my own view of the reality that transpired.

First Objection

The AVF would be very expensive—so expensive that the nation could not afford it.

Rebuttal

The commission countered that the move to the AVF would actually cost less than conscription based on the commission's use of the economic cost as opposed to the budget cost of manning the force. They suggested that the current pay rate for draftees was at least $2 trillion per year less than they would receive if they were employed in the private sector, a cost that would be eliminated by their higher pay as part of the AVF. The commission considered this low pay a form of taxation on those who served. The commission also argued that training costs would decline due to longer initial enlistment periods for volunteers compared to conscripts.

Reality

In addition to arguments about the underlying validity of economic cost versus budget cost, there are ample data points from which to judge the economics of the AVF. Recruiting costs from the DOD alone have risen to near $4 billion per year for full-time recruiters, marketing and advertising, and facilities. This cost does not include enlistment and reenlistment bonuses (I will deal with them later) or other incentives like higher-education programs. Costs are also higher in the AVF because it is generally an older force with more dependents, which causes health-care costs and other dependent obligations to rise. Training costs for initial recruits may, in fact, be lower in the AVF as a result of higher enlistment standards and longer initial enlistment contracts. Attrition rose in the early years of the AVF and has now stabilized around 15 to 20 percent. The impact of the long-term increases of cash and in-kind compensation for the armed forces is reflected in the current discussions of how and where to cut defense spending; personnel costs are on almost every list. In 1973, the Pentagon budget was $81 billion; in 2013, it was approximately $500 billion, a 6 percent per year compounded increase to which personnel costs were a significant contribution. Personnel costs have risen 46 percent over the past decade.

Second Objection

The AVF would lack the flexibility to expand rapidly in times of crisis.

Rebuttal
The commission argued that the National Guard and reserves would be given new and expanded roles in the overall defense posture and would serve as credible backup when necessary. They noted that "preparedness depends on forces in being, not on the ability to draft untrained men." The commission also noted that they were recommending standby draft legislation.

Reality
The commission's rebuttal is correct in that conscription was never viewed as a means to provide trained soldiers for combat quickly. However, even the structure for conscription, the Selective Service System, is in disrepair and untested today, and the current social value system created by forty years without conscription causes some to wonder how effectively the system could be reestablished no matter how real the crisis.

Use of National Guard and reserves as backup has had mixed results since 1973. Their activation during the Vietnam War was rejected by President Johnson, who favored increased draft calls. The first test of the Total Force doctrine under which the National Guard and reserves were integrated into the active components was a failure. The test came in the first Gulf War in 1990–1991. Under the Total Force doctrine, there were five active component divisions composed of two active brigades and one round-out brigade from the National Guard each, thus constituting a full division. None of the round-out brigades were deemed capable of deploying to the Persian Gulf, and none did. The rebuttal argument fared much better during the current Global War on Terrorism, as one third of the forces deployed to Iraq and Afghanistan were guardsmen and reservists who performed well, particularly in combat support and combat service support roles. This level of involvement was driven by the fact that the size of the active force fell from 2.1 million service members to 1.2 million from 1991 to 2002. The requirement did raise questions regarding the sustainability of National Guard and reserve structures given repeated deployments and their impact on reservists, their families, their employers, and their communities. Debate continues as to whether their organizations can maintain their footing as an operational rather than a strategic reserve. Another indicator of the legitimacy of the commission's rebuttal was the alarming result of several tests of the army's inactive reserve pool. Few members were technically obligated to report, those who did were unprepared, and the Pentagon proved reluctant to take meaningful action in response other than to acknowledge grudgingly that the inactive reserve pool was not a viable second level of backing to the active guard and reserve.

In summary, given the current mindset of the American people, the civilian leadership, and the Pentagon after a generation without conscription, to believe that America could quickly gear up for a draft may be optimistic at best and wishful thinking at worst. The credibility of the Selective Service System has declined with time and disuse.

Third Objection

An all-volunteer force would undermine patriotism by weakening the traditional belief that each citizen has a moral obligation to serve his country.

Rebuttal

Compelling men to serve in the military undermines respect for the government. The commission held that "a voluntary decision to serve is the best answer, morally and practically."

Reality

Both the objection and the rebuttal are based on opinions and anecdotes and are difficult to base policy or broad consensus upon. The merit of each is also subject to change over time based on perceived threats, world events, and other factors. **It is noteworthy that four months after the attacks of 9/11, national security was not the most important issue for Americans (the economy was) and the brief increase in patriotism resulting in increased enlistment reverted quickly to the limited-liability patriotism of patriotic rituals at sports events and bumper stickers.** Finally, my informal polling of World War II, Korean War, and Vietnam War draftees and draft-induced volunteers reveals no unpatriotic emotion, resentment, or disrespect for the government as a result of their service. One thread that does emerge from the polling is resentment or concern for the inequality of the Vietnam-era draft.

Fourth Objection

The presence of draftees guards against the growth of a separate military ethos, which could pose a threat to civilian authority, our freedom, and our democratic institutions.

Rebuttal

Eliminating draftees from the force would have no impact on these issues, since the draftees serve at the lowest levels of the military. It is the senior career officers who create policy and drive culture in the military.

Reality

The consistent concerns expressed by writers and pundits over the past decades regarding the estrangement of the US military from the broader society it serves give merit to this objection. The fact that we have fought two wars for ten years while less than 1 percent of the population has had skin in the game is a reality and feeds the fear, ignorance, apathy, and guilt that lead to reluctance to question the military or national security policy. Although the rebuttal is correct that draftees serving in the lower ranks do not set policy, they certainly influence it. For example, would the stop-loss policy have been implemented as readily on the sons and daughters of well-connected, powerful parents as on poor volunteers? Would we be as tolerant of widespread violence against women in the military if the daughter of a member of Congress became a victim? In 1988, Charles Moskos wrote that "whether one's value judgment of the All Volunteer Force, the irreducible fact remains that without a citizen soldier component the most privileged elements of our own youth ... will not be found in the enlisted ranks." After forty years with an all-volunteer force, it is uncommon to find key decision makers in business, academia, the media, or the government who have served in the military.

Fifth Objection

The higher pay would appeal especially to African Americans, who have fewer civilian career options, and thus create a predominately minority force. This development could lead to lower white enlistments and racial tension within the military.

Rebuttal

The commission rejected this objection because it represented paternalism and a reverse discrimination that would deny African Americans an opportunity to pursue employment and training that was attractive to them.

The commission also argued that if, in fact, there were fewer opportunities for African Americans in civilian society, the remedy was to seek equality in the civilian society, not deny African Americans opportunities in the military. Finally, the commission estimated that African Americans would not constitute more than 19 percent of the AVF.

Reality

The commission's estimates of African Americans representation in the AVF were quickly proven to be off the mark. By 1980, 37 percent of the army enlisted force and 32 percent of its new recruits were African American. The trend continued in the army, the largest of the service branches, for more than twenty years as African Americans represented about a third of all enlistees, while nearly half of all female enlistees were African American. African American reenlistment rates are higher than those for white service members in all branches. African American representation in the navy and air force mirrors that in the civilian population, and it is slightly lower in the Marine Corps. The creation of the AVF did not deny African Americans the opportunity to enlist but made enlistment even more attractive because of the higher pay and benefits of the AVF.

The Gates Commission used race as a measure of representation in the military despite its heavy use of economics as a justification for the AVF. An alternative measure of representativeness, such as socioeconomic status, may have led to a different conclusion at the time and a different assessment today. Finally, the commission did not anticipate the increase in the Hispanic population of the United States. Due to immigration and high birth rates, Hispanics have now passed African Americans as our country's largest minority but are generally underrepresented in the military.

Sixth Objection

Those joining the AVF would be from the lower socioeconomic classes and would be motivated to join by financial rewards rather than patriotism. The force would be manned by mercenaries.

Rebuttal

The commission held that the AVF would not differ from the existing force of conscripts and volunteers with regard to socioeconomic class and that the high entrance standards of the AVF would ensure that the disadvantaged would not be overrepresented. They suggested that mercenaries would not suddenly emerge simply because pay and benefits were increased. They buttressed the point by restricting the definition of mercenaries to those who join solely for pay, usually to serve a foreign nation.

Reality

To some extent, the commission's rebuttal that an all-volunteer force would not differ from the existing force of conscripts and volunteers proved to be correct, because the existing force was made up disproportionately of African Americans and the lower socioeconomic classes. The nation's upper classes avoided the draft through a host of exemptions and deferments based on college enrollment, paternity, marital status, and access to resources and advice about how to avoid the draft. Vice-President Dick Cheney, who most would agree is a national security hawk, secured five educational deferments and thus avoided military service completely. In the AVF, the upper classes are similarly underrepresented. Amy Lutz at Syracuse University wrote in a 2008 paper that "therefore, among the working class, those who have served in the military have tended to come from poorer circumstances, while there is low representation of the children of the very rich. Indeed, additional analysis finds that the highest income quartile was significantly less likely to have served than the lowest, while the second and third quartiles were not significantly different from the lowest quartile in their likelihood to serve. In sum, the economic elite are very unlikely to serve in the military."[6] In its June 30, 2011, report *Military Recruitment 2010,* the National Priorities Project presents

---

6 Who Joins the Military? A Look at Race, Class, and Immigration Status", Amy Lutz Syracuse University, Journal of Political and Military Sociology, Vol. 36, No. 2 (winter), 167-188.

data that show an enlisted soldier is 30 percent more likely to come from the third or fourth socioeconomic quintile than from the first socioeconomic quintile.

The second point in the commission rebuttal—that the high admission standards into the AVF would ensure the disadvantaged would not be overrepresented—has also proven to have some merit. Nonetheless, the military has lowered standards for age, education, physical fitness, and moral rectitude when it fell short of volunteers. In summary, those at the highest and lowest ends of the socioeconomic continuum are less likely to serve—the former because they choose not to and the latter because they cannot qualify.

The debate around mercenaries is driven to some extent by how one defines *mercenary*. Webster's Ninth New Collegiate Dictionary defines a mercenary as someone "serving merely for pay or sordid advantage." The commission's strong emphasis on the economics of the force and recommendations for higher pay, benefits, and bonuses provides some justification for the mercenary tag. We continue to use enlistment and reenlistment bonuses and enhanced education benefits aggressively to man the force (I will address this in the next chapter). **The commission's suggestion that mercenaries would not suddenly emerge simply because pay and benefits increased is ironic, since they suggest that higher pay and benefits would increase enlistments.** Higher pay and benefits do not serve to increase patriotism or any other nonfinancial reason to enlist. Whether you label the post-1973 enlistees mercenaries, financial patriots, or a disadvantaged segment of the population, the AVF is manned at the margins through higher pay and benefits. Patriots will enlist without conscription or bonuses.

Seventh Objection

An all-volunteer force would encourage military operations and interventions, leading to an irresponsible national security policy, and would reduce civilian concerns about militarism.

Rebuttal

The commission felt that the fact that the entire force would be volunteers would have no impact on the national command authority's decision to go to war or initiate military actions. They noted that domestic politics, financial costs, and the nature of threats to national security drive such decisions.

Reality

The legitimacy of the objection is somewhat dependent upon the scope of the military operation. Small-scale, brief interventions executed by elite forces or munitions delivered from great distances do not bring risks to ground troops, volunteers, or conscripts. And it is true that low-level military personnel, volunteers or conscripts, have virtually no direct impact on national security policy decisions leading to military action. The objection is more relevant to longer, larger military operations.

Recent events have caused this objection to be reconsidered on several levels. The absence of skepticism and pushback to the Bush administration's decision to invade Iraq on the part of Congress, the media, and the public reflects the separation of the American people from their military. The president's exhortation to the American people to go shopping and pursue their normal lives as a message to terrorists that they have failed to intimidate us, the fact that he asked no sacrifices of the public, and the fact that the press was not allowed to cover the return of dead service members are examples of policies facilitating this estrangement.

Such policies lead to and reinforce the lens of fear, apathy, ignorance, and guilt through which the American public has viewed the wars in Iraq and Afghanistan. They enable the rationalization of casualties, suicides, divorces, and drug and alcohol abuse of service members experiencing a third or fourth combat tour with rejoinders like, "It's unfortunate, but he volunteered. What did he expect?" Would the wars in Iraq and Afghanistan have gone on as long if we had a force of both conscripts and volunteers? Would combatants have had multiple deployments with limited time at home if we could have tapped more than 1 percent of

America's manpower to fight these wars? If so, would the human toll on service members and their families have been reduced?

A final point that informs this objection and the rebuttal is that Congress has abdicated its responsibility to declare war and granted that authority to the president, an application of the unitary executive concept that has dominated national security for decades under presidents of both parties. The last time Congress voted on a formal declaration of war was 1941. All military operations and interventions since then, including the Korean War, the Vietnam War, the first Gulf War, and the wars in Afghanistan and Iraq were initiated and executed without a formal declaration of war by Congress. The absence of a vote gives each congressman the cover of decreased accountability for the casualties, injuries, suicides, and family traumas suffered by American volunteer service members, enabling statements like, "It's the president's war," and (in response to casualties), "He volunteered." Congressional accountability reflected in open debate about declaring war would be a positive step toward reducing fear, apathy, ignorance, and guilt.

Eighth Objection

An all-volunteer force would be less effective, because not enough highly qualified youth would be likely to enlist and pursue military careers. Therefore, the attractiveness of military service would decline, making recruiting more difficult.

Rebuttal
The fact that every service member has chosen to volunteer would make military service more attractive, as the armed forces would be more experienced and enjoy higher morale.

Reality
There is little doubt that the quality of enlistees into the AVF is good. Nevertheless, the military today struggles to man a force of 1.4 million

members while the force stood at 2.4 million in 1973. In 2004–2007 during the wars in Afghanistan and Iraq, the Pentagon was forced to lower enlistment standards to fill the ranks. The minimum quality standard required to enlist tells only half the story; the other half rests in attracting the highly qualified applicants, particularly officers, to which the commission's report referred. The fact is that the military competes for high-quality talent in the information age using industrial-age selection, competition, and retention methodologies. Its civilian competition for highly qualified talent has greater flexibility in starting salaries and selective use of bonuses, faster promotion based on contribution, and pensions that vest after five years. Furthermore, civilian employers do not require new employees to sign a contract to remain an employee for four to six years. As the military becomes more technologically oriented in both war fighting and administration, and as a complex world demands those with the intellectual capacity to develop strategic thinkers, these highly qualified personnel become more critical.

We measure the physical fitness score of every army ROTC cadet but not his or her IQ. The subtle anti-intellectualism persists throughout an officer's career, as those who are selected to attend the army's most elite officer's schooling, the Army War College, are not graded, and academic failure is almost unheard of. The overall system is further weakened by the fact that one can only enter at the bottom (except in some medical fields), precluding fresh ideas, different perspectives, and current skill sets from engaging the system at a level where policy decisions are discussed and made. If, in the middle of his career, Steve Jobs had decided to sell Apple to join the army in response to an overwhelming sense of patriotism, he would have been sworn in as a private. In summary, the military is at a distinct disadvantage in recruiting and retaining highly talented people in a global economy compared to civilian organizations. The AVF gives exemptions to the most talented.

Ninth Objection

An all-volunteer force would cost so much that the nation could not afford it, thus taking funding away from other areas of the defense budget, such as research, development, and acquisition.

Rebuttal

The Gates Commission fell back on the argument of the commission's economists that although the budget costs would be higher, those costs would be more than offset by eliminating the economic costs inherent in conscription in the form of the hidden tax imposed on those forced to serve at below-market rates of pay. They further argued that the overall economy would be more productive with an all-volunteer military. Finally, they argued that the military would demand less manpower using the AVF and thus be more efficient.

Reality

Since 1973, the defense budget has risen steadily. Not just the personnel account but virtually all major accounts in the Pentagon budget have gone up. The largest increases occurred during the Reagan and George W. Bush administrations, and the budget has only recently come under pressure to be reduced, with many in Congress and the defense supply base resisting the reductions. Secretary of Defense Leon Panetta said in 2012 that "the escalating growth in personnel costs must be confronted. This is an area of the budget that has grown by nearly 90 percent since 2001." Even if reductions in spending are implemented, it should be noted that the US defense budget is greater than that of the next fourteen nations' defense budgets combined.

CHAPTER 4 – SAVING THE ALL-VOLUNTEER FORCE

The military compromises to fight a long war the AVF was never intended to fight.

The all-volunteer force instituted in 1973 has worked in that it has provided sufficient manpower at acceptable physical and mental standards to man our forces at acceptable budget levels. The lessons of these past twelve years of war challenge this position and may expose it as an illusion. The Gates Commission made a number of positive assumptions about cost, troop levels, and representativeness in an all-volunteer force that proved at various times to be incorrect, some wildly so. Nevertheless, the AVF model continued to survive and, in the opinion of some observers, thrive. One need go no further than the halls of the Pentagon or some congressional offices to hear the praises of the AVF sung. There were even high-level civilian conferences at the ten-year anniversaries of the AVF in 1983, 1993, and 2003. The conferences published volumes of papers presented by the participants, who often include some of the architects of the initiative in the critical 1965–1973 timeline.

The Gates Commission recommended dramatically increasing the pay of first-term enlistees and that of military personnel at all ranks as a necessary step in order for the AVF to be successful. The commission and Congress also correctly argued that additional resources would have to be devoted to increased recruiting and advertising budgets to attract volunteers. Finally, the Pentagon argued that quality-of-life issues, such as housing, recreational faculties, and medical care, would need to be improved. All of these changes made the transition to the AVF feasible based on what was known at that time. All have been costly.

Just as major changes have occurred in the world since 1973, major changes have occurred within the military and the broader national security landscape. Some changes emerged from policies that the military or Congress initiated, and some were brought on by other forces. All of the factors I will explore served to make the AVF viable, and most were not anticipated by the Gates Commission—they were rabbits pulled unexpectedly out of the hat. The obvious question is this: Are there any more rabbits in the hat, and are the old ones healthy?

Soviet Gift

> The collapse of the Soviet Union allowed the United States to reduce its active military forces by a third. Have we squandered the "Peace Dividend"?

Based strictly on mathematics, one of the principal saviors of the AVF has been the fall of the Soviet Union and its impact on reducing the size of the US active military force. A smaller American force requires fewer enlistees. While the size of the AVF has been reduced by a third since its birth (with the biggest reduction after 1990), the size of the US population has risen by approximately 50 percent since 1975. Neither the Gates Commission nor anyone else in 1970 could have predicted the peaceful fall of the Soviet Empire in 1989.

 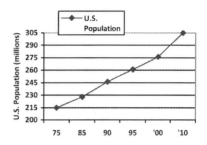

Discussion about whether the AVF could have survived without the benefit of the gift from the Soviets is worthwhile as it relates to the military's fair, efficient, and sustainable structure. Could the Pentagon have recruited and retained a force 33 percent larger than the one it had struggled to man since 1990, and—more importantly, perhaps—at what cost? The peace dividend would have been replaced by an ongoing demand on the treasury. Increases in basic personnel costs would have been linear, and recruiting and retention costs would have been exponential if standards were maintained. This demand on the treasury would have affected the guns vs. butter debate for the nation as a whole. It would have affected Pentagon budget decisions about tradeoffs between personnel costs and other areas, such as weapons procurement, research and development, and infrastructure.

Noncitizens Serving

> We offer the prospect of citizenship to non citizen enlistees who place themselves in Harm's Way to protect the freedom and liberty of 300 million people who decline to protect them. The Roman empire also used this model with tragic results.

Many American citizens are surprised to learn that noncitizens are permitted to serve in the US military and are actively recruited nationwide. Those same Americans are often shocked to learn the number of noncitizens serving in their military; it has varied over the past ten years between twenty-nine thousand and thirty-seven thousand.[7] Put into context, this figure represents two or three army combat divisions or 15 percent of the entire Marine Corps. Since 2001, the United States has granted citizenship to more than thirty thousand service members, and since 2002, the US military has enlisted approximately eight thousand noncitizens per year into the AVF.

On one hand, one may view the policy of recruiting noncitizens into the military as an enlightened immigration practice to give energetic, ambitious, patriotic young people the opportunity to better themselves, become citizens, provide for their families, and secure an education through the GI Bill. Generally, these are immigrants who are at the lower end of the American socioeconomic continuum with limited prospects for upward mobility.

On the other hand, the policy may be viewed as a cynical ploy to take advantage of an underclass by dangling pay, housing, medical benefits, and the chance of accelerated US citizenship in front of them. **You can have all this for simply volunteering to place yourself in harm's way to protect the freedoms and liberties of three hundred million people—freedoms and liberties to which you cannot lay claim as a noncitizen.** Meanwhile, the overwhelming majority of those who claim those freedoms and liberties choose not to protect them. Charles Moskos, a respected sociologist at Northwestern University, summarized this view when he said, "we can't get enough middle class kids to die for our country. This is the next step."

No matter how we view this debate, the issue here is citizenship for service and the fact that eight thousand noncitizens per year enlist in the AVF. This route to citizenship takes four forms. First, during wartime, an immigrant who enlists, whether he or she is documented or undocumented, can apply for expedited naturalization after only one day of service and have the naturalization fee (which ranges from $390 to $675) waived. Furthermore, a person who is subject to a final order

---

7 "US Military Will Offer Path To Citizenship," The *New York Times,* Julia Preston, February 14, 2009.

of removal from the United States is not eligible for naturalization, but this rule does not apply to immigrants who naturalize through military service. Enlistment thus becomes uniquely attractive to noncitizens subject to a final order of removal. If a service member fails to complete his or her term of service honorably, citizenship is revoked—a powerful retention tool. Second, during peacetime, a service member must wait for a full year after enlistment to apply for citizenship; the application fee for citizenship is waived, and the same final order of removal exemption applies, as does the requirement for honorable service. Third, the surviving spouse of a US citizen who died while serving honorably on active duty may apply for naturalization. The surviving spouse is not subject to any requirement of a minimum period of residency in the United States. Finally, citizenship may be granted posthumously to an immigrant serving on active duty if the death was the result of injury or disease caused by or made worse by the war. Posthumous requests for citizenship may be filed by the deceased service member's next of kin or their representative. A grant of posthumous citizenship has no effect on the immigration status of next of kin. It is a symbolic honor bestowed on the deceased service member.

In December 2008, the DOD took the recruitment of noncitizens a step further when it announced a yearlong program to recruit one thousand noncitizen health-care professionals and linguists to serve in the military who did not even have green cards.[8] The only requirements were that they be legal aliens who had resided in the United States for two years and that they undergo security screenings.

It is important to note that legal permanent residents have served in the US military since the Revolutionary War, and since the Civil War more than 660,000 military veterans have become naturalized citizens. Recruiting noncitizens has become more intense in the AVF and has accelerated even more since the War on Terror began in 2001. They have served well with no systemic discipline issues or failures

---

8 "Non-Citizens fight and Die for Adopted Country," *USA Today,* Valerie Alvord, April 8, 2003.

to perform their assigned duties to military standards. In fact, their success rate, measured by completion of entry-level training and the first term of service (generally three or four years), is significantly better than that of citizen enlistees. Therefore, the expanded recruitment and enlistment of noncitizens is an attractive but slippery slope as we struggle to fill the ranks of our AVF. Centuries ago, Rome, the dominant power of its time, employed noncitizens in large numbers in its legions with disastrous consequences. Edward Gibbon wrote in *The Decline and Fall of the Roman Empire* that "The minds of men were gradually reduced to the same level, the fire of genius was extinguished, and even the military spirit evaporated … their personal valor removed, but they no longer possessed the public courage which is nourished by the love of independence, the sense of national honor, the presence of danger, and the habit of command. They received laws and governors from the will of their sovereign, and they trusted for their defense to a mercenary army."

Military Contractors

Substituting highly paid contractors motivated by profit rather than patriotism weakens the military and leads to waste, fraud, and abuse.

Use of military contractors is a well-established practice and first appeared on the American battlefield as early as 1775. Contractors then provided services including feeding, clothing, and transporting a developing army that had little organic equipment and infrastructure. World War I saw less use of military contractors than the Revolutionary War or the Civil War, because it was fought on foreign soil, creating long lines of communication that resulted in limited access to contractor organizations. Additionally, the European theater of operations was relatively well developed. Finally, the establishment of the Quartermaster Corps in 1912 reduced dependence on contractors. It was a completely militarized organization with its own equipment and personnel trained to perform a range of supply and service functions on the battlefield.

Use of contractors tended to stabilize over the period between World War I and the war in the Balkans in 1991–1995 as the chart below shows. The significant aberration in the trend was the Gulf War of 1990–1991. This aberration was the result of a relatively long period of buildup of forces and organic logistical infrastructure in the theater prior to the start of hostilities and the fact that Saudi Arabia was willing and able to provide a substantial sustainment base, which reduced the requirement for US contractors.

Conflict and Period	Ratio of Contractors to Service Members
Revolutionary War (1775–1783)	1:6
Civil War (1861–1865)	1:5
World War I (1917–1918)	1:20
World War II (1941–1945)	1:7
Korea (1950–1955)	1:2.5
Vietnam (1961–1975)	1:6
Gulf War (1990–1995)	1:60
Balkans (1991–1995)	1:1
Afghanistan (2001–present)	1:1
Iraq (2002–present)	1:1

1. Strategic Research Project by LTC Timothy R. Rickert, US Army War College, March 2011

Starting with the war in the Balkans in 1991–1995, there was a marked increase in the ratio of contractors to uniformed service members when America went to war. There are many explanations for this increase, such as increased complexity of weapons systems requiring technicians from the manufacturer, cheap labor available from other nations, contractors supposedly being more efficient, and the need for specialization not available within the DOD. Additionally, there have been a number of directives and programs to expand the use of contractors within the DOD and throughout the federal government. In 1985, the army initiated the Logistics Civilian Augmentation Programs (LOGCAP) to preplan the use of civilian contractors to augment army forces. In 1990, the DOD formally made contractors part of the total force. In 1997, Secretary of Defense William Cohen released his Defense Reform Initiative to reduce "excess" structure and encourage the use of modern business practices. Finally, the *Quadrennial Defense Review Report* of 2001 stated, "only those functions that must be performed by DOD should be kept by the DOD. Any function that can be provided by the private sector is not a core government function. Traditionally, 'core' has been very loosely and imprecisely defined and too often used as a way of protecting existing arrangements." Clearly, a predisposition to contract out functions had emerged.

Although all these explanations and initiatives may have merit, I suspect that the United States has substituted contractors for force structure because as long as we are committed to the AVF concept we cannot recruit and retain a sufficient number of service members to prosecute our nation's wars without contractors. These contractor initiatives have occurred in three principal categories: private security contractors, logistics contractors, and intelligence operations. US Comptroller General David M. Walker reported to the House Subcommittee on Readiness in March 2008 that among the factors that have led to an increase in outsourcing more services in the military were "limitations on the number of authorized full time equivalent positions; unavailability of certain capabilities and expertise among federal employees; desire for operational flexibility; and the need for 'surge' capacity." "Limitations on the number of authorized full-time-equivalent positions" refers to the number of service members Congress is willing to pay for and the military is willing to recruit. Surge capacity is the ability of the military to expand the size of the force quickly, which is difficult to do in the AVF model. All of these factors can be traced back to the AVF either directly or indirectly.

To varying degrees, each of the three categories of contractors present similar problems of contract administration, contractor oversight, control of contractor behavior, and contractor coordination with military organizations. From 1990 to 2003, the population of DOD contracting officers was reduced from 10,000 to 5,500. Nevertheless, a 2009 GAO report states that "The Department of Defense (DOD) is the largest buying enterprise in the world. Since fiscal year 2001, DOD's spending on goods and services more than doubled to $388 billion in fiscal year 2008, and the number of weapons systems programs has also grown." We therefore prepared for a doubling of contract spending by cutting the number of contracting officer professionals in half and eliminated all of the flag and general officer positions from the DOD contracting organization at the same time. It is little wonder and no secret that Congress, the controller general, the special inspector general for Iraq reconstruction, the special inspector general for Afghanistan reconstruction, the DOD, and other government and nongovernment organizations have reported serious cases of waste, fraud, and abuse by DOD contractors. Legislative and policy remedies have been implemented slowly and with mixed effects. The detail and scope of these contractor-related problems and their remedies are beyond the scope of this book. The point is that these issues are far less likely to exist when uniformed service members are performing the tasks now being performed by contractors. I should note that the outsourcing of menial tasks, such as grass cutting and dishwashing, benefits the readiness of our military; problems emerge when tasks expand beyond the menial.

In addition to the doctrinal and high-level problems created by contractors, they present tactical and operational problems in the war zone. First, while civilian contractors are subject to US federal laws, these laws may not be applicable outside the United States. They are not subject to the Uniform Code of Military Justice and thus present a range of problems if they break the law. Furthermore, while they can take instructions, they do not have to take orders. If they choose not to do something, military commanders are limited in what can be done to them; firing is the most severe punishment. Second, contractors can sow dissention and be harmful to military discipline. They are employed by a contractor and do not have to work the hours uniformed service members do and are paid more. They can express views and opinions about military leaders and orders that service members cannot. Third, contracting agencies can recruit above-average service members away from the military by offering higher pay, better working conditions, and more autonomy. Fourth, contractors are civilians and must be protected by the uniformed military, especially when they find themselves in dangerous situations. These events are not uncommon even in cases involving armed private security contractors.

The predisposition to contract would be difficult to change, since contractors can lobby, make campaign contributions, and provide lucrative postretirement opportunities to senior service members. Additionally, there is less political risk to legislators in maintaining the status quo. This status quo is manifest in three areas: armed private security contractors, logistics operations, and intelligence operations. A brief description of each follows.

A 2008 CBO Report states that "contractors also perform some functions, such as security, that have traditionally been reserved for the military." The use of armed private security contractors flies in the face of traditional Western political and military thought, which holds that sovereign states have a monopoly on the use of force and violence exercised through their military and police forces and that when force and or violence is exercised it will be in unquestioned support of the strategic political objectives of the nation. Furthermore, if force and violence is exercised indiscriminately, it is assumed that those who act in that indiscriminate manner will be subject to legal sanctions and punishments. Reality over the past several decades shows that the United States has deviated from these norms. Security contractors are for-profit organizations, not political entities. The American press has reported dozens of alleged abuses by armed private security contractors and the consequences—or absence thereof—imposed as a result of investigations.

Civilian contractors working for DynCorp in the Balkans wars were accused by a fellow employee of participating in a child prostitution and sale ring in that theater. The whistleblower was fired, and later the accused employees were fired. No charges were ever filed. Some of the interrogators involved in the Abu Ghraib scandal were civilian contractors provided by Titan and CACI. None were charged with crimes. However, six junior enlisted soldiers were charged as a result of investigations, tried under the Uniformed Code of Military Justice, and severely punished. In 2007, armed private security contractors employed by Blackwater killed seventeen Iraqi civilians at Nissor Square in Bagdad. The contractors admitted firing on the civilians; none have been successfully tried due to questions of jurisdiction and the applicability of the Uniformed Code of Military Justice, Iraq laws, and US laws. As a result, none have spent a day in prison. All four companies, DynCorp, CACI, Titan, and Blackwater, continued to receive government contracts. Jurisdiction over all contractors, and armed private security contractors in particular, continues to be a problem with which the US Congress, the Department of Defense, and host nations struggle.

Due to their nature—by definition, they are private and deal with security—it is difficult to gather accurate data on individual private security contractors. For the purposes of this book, we do know that in Iraq in 2003 there were approximately ten thousand armed security contractors. In 2004 that number grew to twenty thousand, and by 2007 it was thirty thousand. By March 2009, it had fallen to approximately ten thousand. The AVF benefited from this employment of armed private security contractors in that it was not required to generate at a minimum twenty thousand to sixty thousand more volunteers to execute the mission in Iraq. (The twenty thousand to sixty thousand figure assumes a one-to-one rotation policy, or one year in Iraq followed by one year of recovery.) We substituted armed private security contractors for force structure at the expense of the traditional monopoly on use of force and unity of operational command on the battlefield.

Reducing force structure at the logistical tail of the military, which includes supply, administration, and so forth, rather than the trigger-pulling tooth of combat arms is seductive. It is particularly seductive because it offers bigger opportunities in dollars and force structure than armed private security contractors do. The contract under which Kellogg, Brown, and Root operated in Iraq was estimated to be worth $13 billion. This represents more than two-and-one-half times the total cost of the 1991 Gulf War. In 2010, there were more than 95,000 contractors in Iraq; 24,000 were US citizens. Also in 2010, there were 112,000 contractors in Afghanistan; 16,000 were US citizens. The majority of contractors and the US citizen portion were involved in logistics support rather than security. Like most reductions in force structure, this one does not come without risk.

The most compelling risk is that the US military could lose its capability to execute combat sustainment operations in support of combat operations while relying on a proficiency at negotiating and executing contracts—contracts to do what DOD has historically done internally. The existing predisposition to contract out combined with pressure to maintain the status quo among the American people, Congress, lobbyists, contractors who can make election contributions, and uniformed and civilian DOD decision makers who have no career incentive to rock the boat make this total loss of capability a real possibility.

The expanded use of logistical contractors presents risk beyond the loss of capability in the military. Principal among them are the legal and accountability issues already discussed and shared with security contractors. Integration with military operations in theater is the responsibility of the combatant commander. He can issue orders to military units but not contractors. They are driven by the terms of their contract, which was usually negotiated by a contracting officer seven thousand miles away in the United States and monitored by an undertrained contracting officer representative (usually as an additional duty). This leads to the potential for accountability issues and poor contract execution, waste, fraud, and abuse. Even the current level of logistics-contractor dependence lends itself to potential cost escalation. The free-market defense against cost escalation is muted by cronyism and a very limited number of potential suppliers of the services being contracted.

A critical aspect of integrating logistics contractors is their readiness. The Army's Logistics Civilian Augmentation Program (LOGCAP) contractors are required by contract to be capable of deploying in seventy-two hours, beginning support operations within fifteen days, and of being fully operational within thirty days of deployment. The military continuously monitors the readiness of its organic units, both combat and support, with regard to manning, equipment, and training through monthly readiness reports, inspector general activities, and higher level command oversight. Contractors are not subject to any such inspections or oversight prior to deployment. We learn whether they are ready when it may be too late. Finally, since contractors are for-profit entities, they are subject to work stoppages due to payment disputes with the government or the risk in their area of operation becoming excessive as a result of combat operations.

Although the expanded use of armed private security contractors and contract logistics may be troubling from an operational and doctrinal standpoint, it is not as troubling as contracting intelligence operations. Security and logistics contractors have large numbers of personnel involved and thus have a greater impact on protecting the AVF concept, but they are more transparent and likely to be dramatically reduced when combat operations cease. Use of intelligence contractors is less transparent and more complex, as they embed themselves into every level of intelligence operations from the highest strategic levels, giving input to the President's daily intelligence briefing, briefing field commanders in Iraq and Afghanistan, and gathering human intelligence in war zones. Because of their immersion in day-to-day operations, their system expertise, their support from high-level officials, and the lack of transparency and accountability in many of their contracts, it is unlikely that intelligence contracting will decline any time soon. Inherent government functions and core activities will remain under pressure to be contracted as a result of industry lobbying, campaign contributions, and inertia.

With respect to the AVF, intelligence contracting is more of a quality issue than a quantity issue. The AVF gives a blanket deferment to the best and the brightest who in earlier times would have been more likely to serve either as draftees or as draft-induced volunteers. Today, graduates of our best universities who have the intellectual capacity to develop as intelligence analysts are unlikely to consider the military. Computer science graduates from our best universities are equally unlikely to consider the military. Self-interest and structure inform this reality. Entry-level officers on average were paid $33,940 per year as of 2011. Individual intelligence contractors cost the DOD up to $250,000 per year. Even when highly motivated, capable young people choose to join the military in intelligence functions, they are subject to being lured away by contractors who value their training and security clearances. The contractors offer high salaries, greater autonomy, and the chance for rapid promotion. Contractors made up 51 percent of the Defense Intelligence Agency staff in 2007 and 70 percent of the Pentagon's counterintelligence field activity. The AVF requires not only numbers of volunteers but also volunteers with requisite capabilities; otherwise, in the case of military intelligence it risks being at the mercy of contractors committed primarily to profit rather than operational excellence and patriotism.

Expanded use of contractors to execute functions traditionally executed by uniformed military personnel has served the AVF concept well. As noted above, in 2010 more than 24,000 contractors who were US citizens were serving in Iraq along with 16,000 in Afghanistan, a total of 40,000. Were they there, with all the unique problems and risks that presented, because the AVF concept rendered America unable or unwilling to generate 80,000 to 160,000 more volunteers?

Bonuses: Show Me the Money

> If it's an "All Volunteer Force" why do we pay 18 year olds with no military skills $20,000 just to enlist?

The first real test of the AVF came on the heels of the attacks of 9/11 when America responded by invading both Afghanistan and Iraq under the assumption that the military operations would be brief. We were told that we would be greeted as liberators, small numbers of troops would be required, and that Iraq's oil would pay for the war. When it became clear that the wars would last longer and require significantly more troops than planned for, manning the AVF became a problem that exceeded the expectations of the Rumsfeld Pentagon and the Gates Commission. The question of manning the force in the post-9/11 era was affected by a range of factors that made recruiters' jobs more difficult.

First among the factors was the influence of the wars themselves. After the initial burst of enlistments following the 9/11 attacks, the grim reality of the dangers and costs of war sunk in for the average American, and enlistment fell off to normal rates. As the wars proceeded and casualty rates rose, young Americans and their parents became less enthusiastic about military service, particularly in the army and the Marine Corps. In a nationwide poll of young Americans, 68 percent said that the Global War on Terrorism made them less likely to join the military. The pool of eligible recruits during this period was also constrained by declining high-school graduation rates in the United States. The army's goal is for 90 percent of its recruits to be high-school graduates, but the national graduation rate is between 70 percent and 75 percent. In some large cities it is below 50 percent. For the army, the single best indicator of a recruit succeeding in the first term of enlistment is a high-school diploma.

Emerging trends in the broader society also made recruiting more difficult. Historically, inner cities and urban areas have been rich areas for military recruiting, and many remain so. But the rise of racially and ethnically oriented gangs that can recruit very young members (too young for military service) makes military recruiting more difficult. Affiliation and loyalty to the gang is established early in this battle for human talent; both gangs and the military seek young, fit, mentally able recruits and offer security, opportunity, and affiliation with a strong organization. Often, these young potential recruits, whether gang members or not, have criminal records that disqualify them from military service. The army responded by lowering its standards for high-school graduation and physical fitness and dramatically increasing the number of moral waivers it granted. In February 2008, the *Baltimore Sun* reported that there was "a significant increase in the number of recruits with what the army terms 'serious criminal misconduct' in their background," which included "aggravated assault, robbery, vehicular manslaughter, receiving stolen property, and making terrorist threats." In fact, according to a report by the Palm Center, a California-based military think tank, in 2006 the army approved 901 waivers for felony convictions, up from 411 in 2003. Approximately 10 percent of the moral waivers granted in 2006 were for felony convictions. From 2003 to 2006, waivers for serious criminal history grew from 2,700 to more than 6,000.

A final broad social trend that made military recruiting more difficult in the period was the rapidly increasing portion of the recruiting age population that was overweight or obese. The American Obesity Society reports that forty-nine states have obesity rates above 20 percent and that 30.4 percent of all adolescents age twelve to nineteen are overweight and 15.5 percent are considered obese. Directly related to this issue is its adverse effect on the overall physical fitness of this age cohort relative to previous generations. The army responded by lowering its standards for weight and physical fitness for initial entrance into its ranks.

The measures taken by the military to fill its ranks—lowered standards, moral waivers, more advertising, and appeals to patriotism—had some positive impact on improving recruiting. But the effects fell at the margins and were insufficient to fill the ranks. The game-changing solution was bonuses: money—lots of it—spread over a wide population to significantly impact both enlistments and reenlistments.

All branches of the military, particularly the army, have employed financial bonuses to meet their recruiting goals and achieve their end strength for a long time. Enlistment bonuses have two purposes. One is to expand the pool of potential recruits by enticing those who might otherwise not choose to join the military. The other purpose is known as *channeling,* which is intended to direct those considering military service to choose military occupational specialties (MOS) that are generally less attractive or where the service has the greatest need. Until 2005, channeling was the predominant use of bonuses.

In fiscal year 2005, at the height of the Iraq War, the army failed to meet its recruiting target for the year. This occurred despite the fact that basic military pay rose 10 percent more than that of comparably educated civilians between 2001 and 2006. **In response to the enlistment shortfalls in 2005, a dramatic increase in enlistment bonuses was implemented beginning in 2006. In 2005 the DOD enlistment bonus budget increased from $296 million to $475 million. In 2008 it rose to $611 million, and about 70 percent of army enlistees received a bonus.** The near universal granting of bonuses indicates that the bonus expansion was targeted at expanding the pool of recruits rather than channeling. From 2000 to 2004, the percentage of army enlistees receiving bonuses stabilized around 40 percent except for an increase in 2001 to the 50 percent to 60 percent range. The number of enlistees receiving bonuses peaked in mid-2005 at slightly more than 80 percent.

The DOD and army-wide expenses for enlistment bonuses are noteworthy. Another way to look at the numbers is on an individual basis. From 2001 to 2004, army enlistment bonuses stabilized in the range of $8,000 to $11,000 and fell to the low end of this range in 2004 (briefly dropping as low as $5,600). In 2005, the average bonus jumped to $10,500, and by 2007 it had reached approximately $21,000, peaking in the summer of 2007 at $22,400 when the army implemented its "quick ship" bonuses to ensure that it would make its 2007 contract mission. army enlistment bonuses declined to approximately $18,000 per enlistee by mid-2008, a threefold increase over the 2003–2004 levels. Financial patriotism helped fill the ranks.

There are a number of perspectives from which to judge this policy of expanding enlistment bonuses from 2003 to 2008. A pragmatist might suggest that DOD and army manpower planners did what they had to do in order to man the AVF. A social scientist or economist might argue that substantial sums of money were made available to socioeconomically disadvantaged young people who never would have been able to secure these sums of money through any legal means. A cynic might say that America took advantage of the socioeconomically disadvantaged and bought almost $2 billion of patriotism from 2005 to 2008. We will return to this issue using the framework of fairness, efficiency, and sustainability later in the book. It is noteworthy that a 2010 study by the RAND Corporation estimated that the huge expansion of enlistment bonuses in 2004–2008 resulted in 26,700 high-quality enlistments, representing about 20 percent of high-quality enlistments generated in that period.

The DOD and the army in particular have used reenlistment bonuses to balance their requirement for experienced personnel and those wishing to remain in the military. The overall costs have been relatively stable and reasonable given this limited objective. The selective reenlistment bonus (SRB) program has historically based eligibility on MOS, rank, and seniority. In fiscal year 1999, the army initiated the targeted SRB program in order to entice reenlistment to less desirable locations, such as Korea overseas and Fort Drum, New York, within the continental United States. In 2004, the army initiated the SRB for soldiers deployed to Afghanistan and Iraq and briefly (from September to December 2003) offered a lump sum $5,000 reenlistment bonus to soldiers deployed in Afghanistan, Iraq, and Kuwait. Prior to fiscal year 2005, the army paid half of the reenlistment bonus as a lump sum and spread the remainder over the period of reenlistment through annual payments. In 2005 the army began paying the entire bonus at the time of reenlistment. The mechanics of how individual SRB amounts are calculated is complex, and the formula changes often, but the following table provides a macro view of how the program expanded as the AVF faced its first test:

Year	Percentage of Reenlistments Receiving Bonuses	Total Cost in Millions of Dollars
2000	21.4	105
2001	19.2	110
2002	13.7	90
2003	14.0	103
2004	30.2	143

2005	64.0	506
2006	96.8	708
2007	51.0	535
2008	63.8	686

As the table above shows, there was a dramatic increase in the percentage of soldiers eligible for reenlistment who received bonuses. From the prewar years to 2006 there was almost a fourfold increase in the percentage of reenlistments receiving bonuses. Even more dramatic was the cost of the program. The same cost comparison indicates a sevenfold increase in the program. The previously mentioned 2010 RAND Corporation study estimated that without the SRB program, reenlistments in 2006 would have been 8 percent lower than realized with the bonuses, which would have clearly brought into question the viability of the AVF concept. A final program of note that the army initiated in 2006 was the critical skills retention program, which was targeted at senior noncommissioned officers approaching the twentieth year of service, when they would be eligible for retirement. Although few service members are eligible for the bonus, it is noteworthy because individual participants receive up to $150,000 for a six-year reenlistment. This dramatic expansion of the army's reenlistment bonus program facilitated the next factor to be reviewed here: redeployment policies.

Multiple Redeployments

No horse is so dead that it can't be beaten one more time.

As the institutional army leveraged unprecedented enlistment and reenlistment bonuses to meet its end strength as authorized by Congress, it nonetheless encountered manning problems under the all-volunteer concept. Operational demands for troops exceeded supply based on the army's policy of using a 1:2 deployment ratio—two years of recovery for each year in combat. When, in 2009, President Obama ordered an additional thirty thousand to forty thousand troops to Afghanistan, he deployed practically every available US Army brigade to war, leaving few active component units in reserve in case of an unforeseen crisis emerging in other parts of the world (such as Iran or Korea) and further stressed a force that had seen constant deployment since 2002.

The supply problem senior leaders confronted had three potential solutions. The first option was to reduce demand—tell Congress and our allies that we would need to reduce worldwide commitments and assume risk in some areas, since demand exceeded the supply necessary to maintain the 1:2 deployment policy. The second option was to increase supply—request that Congress authorize and fund a dramatic increase in the army and Marine Corps authorized end strength. The issues with this alternative were whether the services could recruit substantially greater numbers of enlistees and whether a debt-burdened nation could afford the billions of dollars required to do so. Both options presented institutional, political, and fiscal risks for uniformed and civilian policymakers. A third option was to use the forces available more often and allow them less time off the battlefield for rest and recovery. The decision makers choose option three.

The option chosen in the scenario above was the same one generally chosen throughout the wars in Iraq and Afghanistan. The one exception came in 2004, when Congress authorized the army and Marine Corps to increase their end strengths by twenty thousand and three thousand respectively. This option was chosen in 2009 despite the army's stated 1:2 deployment policy and despite the fact that by 2009 the devastating effects of repeated long deployments on soldiers and their families were well known. Many of the solders in this cohort of thirty to forty thousand troops would be deploying on their third or fourth combat tour. The decision also seemed to be in conflict with the values of the 2009 Army Posture Statement, which said, "we remember that the Army's most precious resources are our dedicated soldiers, the families, and the Army Civilians who support them." A cynic may balk at this statement in light of the deployment decision and suggest that a more accurate statement might have read, "No horse is so dead that it can't be beaten one more time." Lt. Gen. Thomas P. Bostick, the army's deputy chief of staff, stated in 2010 that 10 percent of solders in a brigade combat team were nondeployable for medical reasons in 2007, and that number rose to 14.5 percent in 2010. He projected that the medically nondeployable would rise to 16 percent in 2012. He also noted that more than nine thousand soldiers were in the army's wounded warrior program. Whether dead or alive, the horse had experienced numerous beatings.

In October of 2011, Sgt. First Class Kristoffer B. Domeij was killed in Afghanistan by a roadside bomb. He was assigned to the army's Seventy-Fifth Ranger Regiment. He was on his fourteenth deployment and had spent more than forty-eight months in Iraq and Afghanistan since joining the regiment in 2002. Rangers assigned to the regiment serve intense three- to four-month combat tours as opposed to the longer tours of conventional troops. He is survived by a wife and two young daughters. Many people, learning this, might note that he volunteered; many others would question the judgment of an institution that would facilitate these circumstances.

Although Sgt. First Class Domeij's deployment history represents the extreme end of soldier redeployment patterns, it represents the extreme of a nevertheless alarming larger pattern. As of 2010, 31 percent of active-duty enlisted soldiers in the army were serving their second combat deployment, 12 percent a third combat tour, and 4 percent their forth (or greater) combat tour. The cycles of combat have been so long and so frequent that through 2010 nearly thirteen thousand soldiers spent three to four cumulative years in combat in Iraq and Afghanistan. Approximately five hundred soldiers spent more than four years in combat. Cumulatively, 47 percent of army personnel were deployed on their second or greater combat tour. The physical, mental, and emotional strain of long and repeated exposure to combat is what makes these wars different. Pulitzer Prize–winning Civil War historian James McPherson said, "what is exceptional … is the repeated deployments." He notes that the average Civil War tour of duty was about two-and-a-half years and goes on to say, "these [current deployments in Iraq and

Afghanistan] may take a greater physical and psychological toll than a single deployment, even if the latter is longer."[9] I will deal in detail in the next section with these effects.

Stop-Loss

The All Volunteer Force resorts to a "back door draft".

One of the most controversial enablers of repeated deployments of soldiers during the wars in Iraq and Afghanistan is stop-loss. According to section 12305 of title 10 of the United States Code, the president, after declaring a national emergency or presidential call-up, may "suspend any provision of law relating to promotion, retirement, or separation applicable to any member of the armed forces determined to be essential to the national security of the United States, and (2) to determine, for the purpose of said section, that members of the armed forces are essential to the national security of the United States."

President George H.W. Bush first used the authority on August 22, 1990, when he delegated the authority to his secretary of defense. On September 19, 2001, Secretary of Defense Donald Rumsfeld delegated stop-loss authority to each of the military services. Stop-loss was rarely used before 9/11 but quickly became controversial as two views of the policy clashed. The Pentagon, in the fiscal year 2009 Defense Authorization Bill Senate Amendment, commented, "Stop Loss should be accepted as a national response that is legitimate, necessary, and expected." Members of Congress, much of the American public, and many soldiers and their families, on the other hand, felt that stop-loss was a backdoor draft totally inconsistent with the principle of an all-volunteer force.

Stop-loss restricts soldiers from voluntarily separating from the army at the end of their commitment if the unit to which they are assigned is

---

9 Military Times, "Troops' deployment burden unprecedented," Gregg Zoroya (USA Today), January 13, 2010.

deploying to Iraq or Afghanistan. Enlistees in the armed forces receive a standard contract that obligates them to a total of eight years of military service, some portion of which is usually in inactive-duty status after separation from the active force. Following separation from the active force, soldiers can elect to be assigned to the Selected Reserve or the Individual Ready Reserve to complete any remaining time of their eight-year commitment. All three components of the army (active, reserve, and National Guard) are subject to stop-loss.

Soldiers with separation dates that fall within ninety days of their deployment date or mobilization date, through the deployment (deployments currently last twelve months in Iraq and Afghanistan), and for a maximum of ninety days following the deployment can be subject to stop-loss. Since 2002, more than 120,000 soldiers from all three components of the army have had their active service extended by stop-loss. In early 2007, Secretary of Defense Robert Gates directed all of the military services to submit plans to minimize stop-loss in response to Congressional and public opposition to this backdoor draft and the threat it posed to the concept of the AVF. Ironically, after Secretary Gates issued his directive, the use of stop-loss actually increased in the army in response to the surge period of 2007–2008. Stop-loss is currently not being used as a means to satisfy deployment requirements, but the authority remains to reinstitute the policy if operational demands require it. Also remaining is the legacy of distrust on the part of soldiers and their families for their senior leaders and the question the policy raises regarding the viability of the AVF.

This legacy of distrust as a result of the military's need to provide a deployable force to the war zone when volunteers were in short supply was fueled by two other policy decisions. First, despite the fact that the military has strict regulations that outline standards for physical fitness and weight control, the physical fitness test or meeting the body weight standard were not part of the criterion for deployment into harm's way, but marksmanship, dental health, and other measures were. The Reserve and National Guard, which represented up to 40 percent of the troops in Iraq and Afghanistan, were most affected by the policy, as they struggled with these individual fitness issues long before 9/11. For obvious reasons, the military does not compile data on the enforcement of these policies. Before I retired in 2006, I asked the senior cadre at three US bases responsible for final preparations of Reserve and National Guard soldiers before they were deployed to Iraq and Afghanistan for their best estimate of what portion of soldiers failed to meet physical fitness or weight standards. Their response was 15 to 20 percent. The policy thus sent 15 to 20 percent of the deploying soldiers from the Guard and Reserve into harm's way even though they were unable to meet individual fitness requirements that, by regulation, would have subjected them to discharge. Standards were compromised to protect the all-volunteer concept.

Another alarming compromise military leaders made to deal with potential deployment shortfalls at the height of the Global War on Terrorism is the way it dealt with gay and lesbian service members subject to discharge under Don't Ask Don't Tell. Combatant commanders needed soldiers, and not enough were available, so enforcement was selective. The Pentagon justified DADT by arguing that the presence of openly gay or lesbian service members in its ranks would adversely affect morale, cohesion, and discipline. Nonetheless, when the first Gulf War began in 1991, the Pentagon announced that the discharge of gays and lesbians could be deferred until they were no longer needed. "Any administrative procedure is dependent on operational considerations of the unit that would administer such proceedings," said Lieutenant Commander Ken Satterfield, a Pentagon spokesman.

Three days after the terrorist attacks of 9/11, President Bush signed an executive order initiating stop-loss. The order allowed but did not require each service to halt DADT discharges. The navy and air force, under less strain to fill their volunteer ranks and deploy troops, continued discharges under DADT. The army and Marine Corps, experiencing pressure to fill their ranks, effectively suspended DADT discharges, a clear compromise of the "morale, cohesion, and discipline" argument. A September 19, 2001, article in the *San Francisco Chronicle* quoted a Pentagon spokesman as saying that while "administrative discharges (medical, hardship, suitability) could continue under Stop-Loss, commanders would be given enough latitude in this area to apply good judgment and balance the best interest of the service, the unit and the individual involved." Note that the service and the unit would "apply good judgment," not the individual involved.

Dr. Nathanial Frank notes in a 2007 white paper a Congressional Research Service finding that "as a result of these policies and laws, the situation that arises during a time of deployment places homosexuals in a no win situation. They are allowed or ordered to serve at the risk of their own lives with the probability of forced discharge when hostilities end if their sexuality becomes an issue. By deploying suspected homosexuals with their units, the services bring into question their own argument that the presence of homosexuals seriously impairs the accomplishment of the military mission." Standards were compromised to save the AVF. Dr. Frank later states in the white paper, "in fact, there is no question that the military delays and neglects gay discharges during the current wars in the Middle East." Noting that these wars began in 2001, the pattern of DADT discharges since 1994 supports his position:

Year	DADT Discharges
1994	617
1995	772
1996	870
1997	1,007
1998	1,163
1999	1,046
2000	1,241
2001	1,273
2002	906
2003	787
2004	668
2005	742

2006	612
2007	696
2008	715
2009	489
2010	261

Better Living through Chemistry

The military medical community compromised itself to "conserve the fighting strength" of the military by its wholesale prescription of psychotropic drugs.

The effect of stop-loss on repeated deployments and its support of the all-volunteer model have been well defined in terms of time frame, legislative authority, and policy. A more troublesome and less well-defined enabler is the dramatic increase in the use of prescription psychotropic drugs to treat service members suffering from anxiety, depression, PTSD, and other psychiatric conditions. The use of these powerful drugs may impair the service members ability to function and delays or denies the access to more comprehensive treatment. The use of drugs in American military history is not new—rum in the Revolutionary War, morphine in the Civil War, and various amphetamines in World War II and Vietnam. "Prior to the Iraq War, soldiers could not go into combat on psychiatric drugs, period. Not very long ago, going back maybe 10 or 12 years, you couldn't even go into the armed services if you needed any of these drugs, in particular stimulants," said Peter Breggin, a New York psychiatrist who has written widely about psychiatric drugs and violence. "But they've changed that … I'm getting a new kind of call right now, and that's people saying the psychiatrist won't approve their deployment unless they take psychiatric drugs." In fact, Colonel Elspeth Cameron Ritchie, a psychiatrist in the office of the army surgeon general, acknowledges that the expanded prescription of psychiatric drugs for combat troops represents a change in deployment policy.

"Twenty years ago we weren't deploying soldiers on medications," she stated. Soldiers deploying today often do so while taking an array of prescription drugs. The Pentagon explained the change in practice in late 2006, noting that there are "few medications that are inherently disqualifying for deployment." She also stated that military officials have concluded that many medicines introduced since the Vietnam era can be used safely in combat zones, particularly antidepressants and sleeping pills, and that small doses of Seroquel, an antipsychotic, can help treat nightmares, even though the drug is not approved for the treatment of nightmares.[10]

There is a disturbing link between the motto of the US Army Medical Department, which states that the military physician's duty is to "conserve the fighting strength" of the army and 2007 deployment statistics in an army report that showed about 12 percent of the combat troops in Iraq and 17 percent of those in Afghanistan were taking prescription antidepressants or sleeping pills. **In March 2010, Senator James Webb said the apparent increase in prescriptions is "on its face, pretty astonishing and troubling."[11] It is particularly troubling because the soldiers to whom the drugs were prescribed were screened for physical, emotional, and psychological well-being prior to their enlistment.**

The scope of the use of prescription psychiatric drugs in the military is astounding. The *Army Times* reported on March 17, 2010, that "one in six service members is on some form of psychiatric drug." The scope of the issue is also apparent from Defense Logistics Agency records indicating that it spent $1.1 billion on common psychiatric and pain medications from 2001 to 2009 and that the use of psychiatric medications overall rose 76 percent. Antidepressants (along with anticonvulsants) are the most common mental health medications prescribed to service members, and their use rose 40 percent during the 2001–2009 period. It was the only drug group to show a decrease in

---

10 "Prescription Pill Dependency Among American Troops is on the Rise," *Men's Health,* Melody Peterson, May 19, 2009.

11 Troops being prescribed more drugs for mental disorders", Bill Bartel, The Virginian- Pilot, March 28, 2010.

spending from $49 million in 2001 to $41 million in 2009 due to the emergence of less expensive generic versions. Anticonvulsant drugs are among the most commonly prescribed psychiatric medications. Annual orders for these psychiatric medications rose about 70 percent, while spending increased from $16 million to $35 million per year. There were even larger increases in antianxiety drugs and sedatives, such as Valium and Ambien; orders shot up 170 percent, and cost rose from $6 million per year to $17 million per year. The largest increase came in the prescription of antipsychotic medications, such as Seroquel and Risperdal, with orders up more than 200 percent and costs rising from $4 million per year to $16 million per year.[12]

Of particular concern to some military medical professionals is off-label usage. As many as 60 percent of veterans receiving prescriptions for antipsychotics received them for conditions for which the drugs were not officially approved according to a 2009 study by the Veteran's Administration. Once a drug is approved by the FDA, it can be prescribed by doctors for any reason they think is reasonable. Drug companies have played a role in the expanded use of their products by the military by aggressive promotion and downplaying their addictive potential. The companies' reach is demonstrated by their relationship with the Association of Military Surgeons of the United States. The companies (as many as eighty of them) set up booths in the convention hall of their annual meetings to promote their products, help defray the cost of the convention, and fund cash prizes to military and federal doctors, all of which is legal.

As disturbing as it might be that we are sending young service members into war zones with prescription psychotropic drugs that the FAA would not allow commercial airline pilots to take, it is explainable. The military (and the army and the Marine Corps in particular) needed to generate sufficient deployable strength to meet wartime requirements. Soldiers and Marines had significant mental health problems. The

---

12 "Medicating the Military," *Army Times,* Andrew Tilghman and Brendan McGarry, March 17, 2010.

military medical system lacked sufficient psychologists, psychiatrists, counselors, and social workers. Drugs were readily available and promoted by drug manufacturers, and the military medical community changed its longstanding policy of not deploying troops into war zones while they are taking psychotropic drugs. The problem is solved without political or public debate regarding ethics or consequences, and the all-volunteer concept is supported through chemistry. **A troubling insight into this explanation is exhibited in a comment from General Peter Chierelli, the army vice–chief of staff, who was quoted by the *New York Times* on February 21, 2011, as saying, "I'm not a doctor, but there is something inside that tells me the fewer of these things we prescribe, the better we'll be." General Chierelli is not a doctor, but he was the second highest ranking officer in the entire United States Army, and the prescription of the drugs to which he refers went on unabated, ostensibly to conserve the fighting strength of the army.**

One Weekend a Month, Two Weeks in the Summer—Really?

Because the Pentagon was unable or unwilling to expand the active force, the Reserve and National Guard were forced to play a role they were not intended or organized to play.

The tradition of our military reserve components goes back to the Revolutionary War and the militias that were formed in each state, which later became the alternative to the large standing army that concerned many of the founding fathers. These militias matured into the National Guard and reserve components of the service branches. Along the way many things changed, but few ever envisioned the reserve components being employed as heavily and repeatedly as they have been over the past ten years absent a declared total mobilization. In fact, the Gates Commission saw the reserve component as a special problem and suggested that approximately 113,000 paid positions in the reserve structure could be eliminated without significantly affecting reserve effectiveness. The commission went on to say that manpower shortfalls in the reserve components were not a threat to national security. The Gates Commission, consistent with its economic orientation, saw participation in the reserve components as having the potential to be a significant part-time job. The thinking at the time was that even an undermanned, poorly equipped, and poorly trained reserve component could act as a bridge between the immediate deployment of active forces and the influx of troops as the result of a standby draft in the event of a national emergency.

During the early years of the AVF, reserve-component readiness and capabilities suffered as a result of congressional funding constraints and the loss of draft-induced enlistments into the reserve ranks. During the Vietnam War, it was the policy of the Johnson administration to employ ever increasing draft calls to satisfy troop requirements rather than mobilize and deploy the reserve components. This policy was politically motivated, as Johnson felt that mobilizing the reserves would expose the scope of the US commitment to the American people and alienate a segment of the electorate that he was loath to upset. Thus, reserve and National Guard enlistment became a way for the resourceful, well connected, or well off to avoid service in Vietnam, instead serving one weekend a month and two weeks in the summer. Many national security experts assert that the AVF was neither suited nor intended to fight a protracted war requiring multiple deployments, and the reserve components were the least suited to serve in protracted engagements.

Nevertheless, the reserve components became a viable and ready source of manpower to meet the needs of combatant commanders in Iraq and Afghanistan. Prior to 2001, the reserve was seen as a strategic reserve that would have time to be alerted, trained, and deployed in an emergency. It was further assumed that a reservist might deploy once in his or her career. The 2006 *Quadrennial Defense Review* rationalizes the change to an operational reserve by stating,

> The traditional, visible distinction between war and peace is less clear at the start of the 21st century. In a long war, the United States expects to face large and small contingencies at

unpredictable intervals. To fight long wars and conduct other functions contingency operations, joint force commanders need to have more immediate access to the Total Force. In particular, the Reserve Component must be operationalized so that select reservists and units are more accessible and more readily deployable than today. During the Cold War, the Reserve Component was used appropriately, as a "strategic reserve", to provide support to Active Component Forces during major combat operations. In today's global context, this concept is less relevant.

Presto: the concept of the reserve components in the AVF changed as soon as the AVF itself was at risk.

This new operationalization of the reserve components had profound effects on individual service members. In the decade following 9/11, approximately 240,000 members of the National Guard and 170,000 reservists have been deployed at least once; 80,000 National Guard personnel and 65,000 reservists twice; 25,000 National Guard personnel and 20,000 reservists three times; and 12,000 National Guard personnel and approximately the same number of reservists four or more times. At one point these reserve components made up 40 percent of the total fighting force in Iraq and Afghanistan according to the Reserve Officers Association. Since 2001, more than 310,000 reserve-component soldiers with children have been deployed; more than 46,000 of those were deployed three times or more.[13]

The active component was stressed to provide sufficient troops, but the stress on the reserve components was even greater. Dr. David Chu, undersecretary of defense for personnel and readiness, testified before the Commission on the National Guard and Reserve in 2010 that "ultimately, the cross cutting question in my judgment is really a question about how frequently should reserve personnel be asked

---

13 "Changing of the Guard: A Look Back at 10 Years of War," The Medill National Security Journalism Initiative, Caitlin O'Neil, February 14, 2012.

to serve. They are reserve personnel. They are not active duty. It's a different status, different set of benefits, different set of rules, different expectations. They do have a civilian career, we need to respect that." It appears that the answer to Dr. Chu's question may be that they will be asked to serve as long and as often as required—or until we break the force. Reducing requirements and conscription were not considered as options.

In response to the question of how long and how often to deploy the reserve components, policymakers and senior military leaders focused on issues of predictability, suggesting that knowing when a unit was to be mobilized and deployed far enough in advance would somehow make things better not only for the Pentagon but also for reserve-component service members, their families, and their employers. The response to the predictability issue was the army force generation (ARFORGEN) model, which would have reserve-component deployments limited to one year with five years between deployments, a 1:5 ratio. Much of the reserve components have been deployed at a 1:3 to 1:4 ratio over the past ten years. Many uniformed observers believe that the earliest the 1:5 ratio will be achievable is 2014. This means that the best case is that after 2014, the average reserve-component service member can expect to be deployed one out of every six years; during these deployments, they will still be separated from their families, civilian careers, and communities. The ARFORGEN model has some problems at both the institutional and individual levels.

At the institutional level, one problem is that during the five-year nondeployed period, the National Guard or reserve unit is expected to train at progressively higher levels. This requires equipment at the unit's home station that is not available because it has been sent to already deployed units or left in theater after the unit's last deployment. Reserve-component units throughout the DOD are short of critical equipment, and billions of dollars will be required to get units to minimum readiness standards in an austere fiscal era. This situation raises an additional concern as to the ability of National Guard units to execute their state mission of emergency response and disaster relief. Similarly, nondeployed units have reached an unprecedented low readiness state for personnel, because individual service members have been transferred to deploying units in order to meet minimum standards set by combatant commanders, a classic application of robbing Peter to pay Paul.

At the individual level, the predictability answer presented by the ARFORGEN model generates two questions for civilian employers (or potential employers) of reserve-component service members and the service members themselves. First, imagine that a hiring manager or decision maker in a civilian organization is considering two equally qualified candidates for a position or a promotion. One of them will be lost to him for one out of every six years, and he will have to replace that candidate for that year and reinstate him upon his return as if he had never left (as required by law), at which point he will have to find a way to deal with the extra person he had to bring on for the year. Why would he hire the reserve-component service member? Given a choice, the rational decision maker will not hire or promote the reserve-component service member. As Mr. Spock on *Star Trek* would say, "It would be illogical." This problem is even more serious for small businesses and self-employed reservists. Second, given the skyrocketing cost of health care for most American employers, if an employer could choose between two equally qualified candidates for hire, one of whom was a service member, why hire the service member knowing that between 20 and 30 percent of Iraq and Afghanistan veterans suffer from PTSD and that this condition could add to already troubling health-care costs? What is the rational choice?

In an effort to shore up the reserve component of the AVF, the DOD has thrown lots of money at the problem. Army National Guard reenlistment bonuses grew from $27 million in 2004 to $308 million in 2006. Similarly, reenlistment bonuses for the army reserve went from $3 million to $140 million in the same period. Between 2004 and 2006, the cost of enlistment bonuses for the National Guard rose from $74 million to $174 million, and the cost of Army Reserve enlistment bonuses rose from $35 million to $71 million.

I will deal with the effects of this deployment policy in the next chapter. In closing this section, I acknowledge that the reserve components have made an extraordinary contribution to the prosecution of the wars in Iraq and Afghanistan. The sacrifices of families, employers, and communities have been unprecedented, and Americans have generally recognized all these sacrifices. But I must note in closing that for every father, mother, son, daughter, brother, or sister deployed as a reserve-component service member for a second or third time, there were many fully qualified eighteen- to twenty-four-year-olds who chose not to become part of an all-volunteer force and went on with their lives while some of those who deployed lost theirs. One can only speculate as to why people and nations make the choices they do.

Women in the AVF

> Women now represent 14% of the force; up seven fold since 1970. Some may see this as great progress others would say they are underrepresented since women are fifty percent of the civilian population. Where participation goes from here will depend on how the military deals with combat exclusion and sexual violence.

In 1997 Goldie Hawn played the title role in the movie *Private Benjamin,* a bewildered, feckless army recruit looking for a way to right her life. The movie was entertaining but did not come close to accurately portraying army life or army recruits. The Gates Commission's view of the role women would play in the AVF was equally deficient. The commission's 1971 vision may have been influenced by the fact that the 2 percent cap on women in the military was only lifted in 1967, the same year that the caps on promotions of women above pay grade 03 (the pay grade of a captain in the army, air force, and Marines and of a lieutenant in the navy) were removed and women became eligible for permanent promotion to pay grade 06 (that of a colonel in the army, air force, and Marines or a captain in the navy). Until 1971, servicewomen who became pregnant were subject to discharge. In retrospect, it is almost unbelievable that the Gates Commission gave so little thought to the role women might have in the success of the AVF, since each woman volunteer reduces the requirement for a male volunteer, and women represented a huge pool of untapped potential. In fact, William Meckling, the staff director of the Gates Commission, was shocked at allegations of the oversight in 1983 and said, "My shock led me to canvass my files in search of contradictory evidence. I could find no record anywhere that we seriously considered the question of expanding the number of women in uniform."[14] And expand it did across a host of dimensions, demonstrating that one of the largest single contributors to the success of the AVF was not seriously considered by the commission that unanimously recommended its adoption.

Today women represent more than 14 percent of the active-duty force, up dramatically from 1.6 percent in 1973 when the AVF came into being. The rise has been dramatic and steady since the recruiting services began to focus resources on female accessions in the early- to mid-1970s. The chart below depicts the increase of women in the total force:

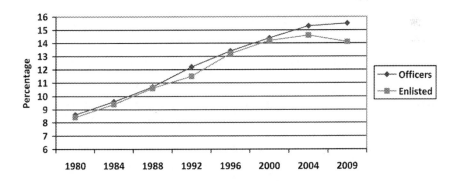

Women's contributions to the success and perhaps the survival of the AVF can be considered in the absolute terms displayed above but also in relative terms. If the 2 percent cap that existed until 1967 had remained in place, the services would have had to recruit 170,000 more

---

14 William H. Meckling "comment on 'Women and Minorities in the All-Volunteer Force," in Rodger and G.Thomas Sicilia William Bowman, ed., "The All-Volunteer Force After A Decade: Retrospect And Prospect", NewYork: Pergmon-Brassey's, 1986. Page 112

male volunteers to man today's military. In the reserves and National Guard, women represent an even larger part of the military: 17.6 percent as of September 30, 2011. In the Air Force Reserve, women made up 26.6 percent of the force and in the Army Reserve 21.6 percent of the force. The Marine Corps Reserve lagged behind the others at 5.7 percent. Given the role that the reserve components have played in Iraq and Afghanistan, is it conceivable that they could have succeeded without the expanded contribution of women?

The contribution of women in modern combat operations did not begin in Iraq and Afghanistan. In Vietnam (which laid the groundwork for the AVF) more than 7,000 women served; 170 served in Grenada; 770 in Panama; 41,000 in the Persian Gulf War; 1,000 in Somalia; 1,200 in Haiti; and more than 16,000 in Bosnia and Kosovo. During World War I, World War II, and the Korean War, there is strong evidence that women participated in the military in even larger numbers—33,000; 400,000; and 120,000 respectively. Although many served in medical, administrative, and support roles, it should be noted that three military nurses received the Distinguished Service Cross in World War I. More than two hundred military nurses died while serving in Europe and the Pacific in World War II, sixteen of them from enemy fire, and eighty-five were prisoners of war. And in Korea, seventeen female service members were killed, and fifty-seven army nurses arrived at Pusan within seventy-two hours of the start of the landing.[15]

While the overall increase in women's participation in the AVF is encouraging, there are a number of trends that may be of concern now and in the future. One is that African American women are enlisting in the military at much higher rates than their white counterparts. African American servicewomen currently represent nearly a third of female service members, nearly twice their percentage in the US civilian population. White women represent 78 percent of the civilian female population but only 53 percent of the women in the military.

---

15 *Women in the Military*, Seventh Edition, Women's Research and Education Institute, Captain Lory Manning, USN (Retired), November 2010.

African American men constitute about 16 percent of the military, approximately equal to their representation in the civilian population. There are no clear answers to why this disparity in the propensity to enlist exists. But it does turn us back to the concern expressed by the Gates Commission regarding overrepresentation of African Americans in an all-volunteer force. Two questions arise: Is this disparity good for the AVF, and can this level of recruitment of African American women be sustained?

Two policy issues internal to the DOD (in addition to external factors including civilian unemployment) will influence whether the military can sustain and even increase the participation of women in the AVF. First is the combat exclusion rule, which has placed a ceiling on women's advancement through the ranks, and, second is sexual violence in the military.

Notwithstanding the impressive rise of women's participation in the AVF over the past forty years (from approximately 2 percent of the force to 15 percent), women represent 50 percent of the recruiting pool. One might therefore argue that they are underrepresented and represent a huge opportunity to support the AVF in terms of the quantity and quality of recruits, both officer and enlisted. A fundamental barrier to exploiting this opportunity is the current policy that restricts how and where women are allowed to serve and fight for their country based solely on their gender. Current combat exclusion policy represents discrimination that is illegal in any other institution in American society.

In entertaining the question of whether the AVF is fair, efficient, and sustainable, one could argue that women do join the military in historically high numbers despite this discriminatory policy. In rebuttal, one might ponder how many highly qualified women do not choose military service at all or choose to not reenlist because of this policy and its impact on their assignment options and career advancement. In early 2013, Secretary of Defense Leon Panetta announced steps to dramatically mitigate the adverse effects of the combat exclusion policy. His directive moved the issue from the theoretical to the operational with more questions than answers for the foreseeable future. Therefore, this discussion of the issue is relevant as the services operationalize his directive.

The current combat exclusion policy has roots going back to World War II, when the army sought ways to bring women onto active service and established the Women's Army Corps (WAC), which gave women the same pay and benefits and military status as men but excluded women from any weapons training or tactical experience or assignments that required weapons. Throughout the 1970s, the number of women serving in the military dramatically increased, prompting the formation in 1972 of the Women in the Army Policy Review Group to deal with policy issues related to professional development and combat readiness. Among the issues engaged was the safety of female soldiers related to their proximity to danger on the battlefield. In response, the DOD issued its Risk Rule policy in 1988. The Risk Rule stated that women would not be assigned to positions where they were likely to be exposed to capture, direct combat, or hostile fire. The asymmetric battlefield of counterinsurgency has presented unique challenges to the policy's execution.

Today's combat exclusion law derives from the 1994 National Defense Act, which provides that the secretary of defense is authorized to determine where women should best serve but that he must conform to strict timelines in informing Congress before making any changes in exiting policy. Much of the debate today regarding combat exclusion focuses on the army's 1992 publication of Army Regulation 600-13, Policy for the Assignment of Female Soldiers. The policy states that female soldiers are allowed to serve in any specialty or position "except in those specialties, positions, or units (battalion size or smaller) which are assigned a routine mission to engage in direct combat, or which collocate routinely with units assigned a direct combat mission."

In addition to the broad policy issues of combat exclusion and whether it should be abandoned or sustained, the policy presents several current issues in its implementation at the tactical or operational level. First, the type of war in which the United States has most recently been involved and is most likely to be involved in in the future is an asymmetric counterinsurgency with no front lines and no rear areas; the entire area of operations is at risk to any US service member (man or woman) within range of an IED, suicide bomber, "green on blue" attack,[16] or ambush. Second, organizational changes initiated by the army in 2004 to create Brigade Combat Teams (BCTs) of three to four thousand soldiers that are self-sustaining require that logistics and other support functions previously assigned to division levels now be integrated into BCTs. Women are heavily represented in these support functions, creating practical and ethical dilemmas for commanders balancing compliance with the combat exclusion policy and mission accomplishment. Third, cultural realities in Iraq and Afghanistan have dictated that US servicewomen integrate deeply into combat operations well below the battalion level to search indigenous females, provide medical treatment to injured females, and secure intelligence from female sources. The military tiptoes around the policy by attaching rather than assigning these servicewomen to these duties and units but does so with such regularity that there is a well-known term for them: *lionesses.*

At the high national policy level, the arguments for and against the combat exclusion policy are driven by myth, traditional values, anecdotal experience, and changes to women's roles in the broader society. Change is difficult and carries with it risk. I should note that many of the same arguments for and against opening ground combat positions also were offered as we considered opening air and naval positions. Women are succeeding today in those positions.

There are three principal arguments in favor of the current combat exclusion policy. First is the idea that the reason men fight is to protect women and their traditional roles as mothers and the culture of femininity. The fact that thousands of civilian women have been killed and wounded in Iraq, Afghanistan, Bosnia, and Rwanda and that hundreds of US servicewomen have similarly sacrificed in Iraq and Afghanistan informs this position. A second concern is that male combat

---

[16] An attack by host-nation service members on American or allied forces.

soldiers could have greater difficulty dealing with female casualties than male casualties, thus reducing readiness and combat effectiveness. The reaction of US soldiers in noncombat units to servicewomen's losses in their units or of sailors to female sailor losses on the USS *Cole* indicates that service members' reactions to causalities in their units or ships are gender neutral; all losses are tragic. Third, women serving in combat units would be subjected to capture, torture, imprisonment, and rape. Due to the nature of the wars we are fighting today, any woman in the theater of operation is subject to these risks, as demonstrated by the experiences of Jessica Lynch and others. One should also note that US servicewomen who served in Iraq and Afghanistan were more likely to be raped by a US serviceman than to be killed by the enemy (I will address sexual violence in the military later). In summarizing the protecting-the-women argument, one should also acknowledge the possibility that what is being protected is the male ego in that armed combat is a means for men to prove their manhood. If women are allowed to participate and perform well, this myth is jeopardized.

A second argument in defense of the combat exclusion policy is that the American people are not prepared to see female combat fatalities or serious injuries in large numbers. I have already touched on the issue but would repeat that we have seen hundreds of female war casualties over the years with no mass revulsion to this point. We have also seen women with serious permanent war injuries and amputations, and there has been no revulsion based on gender. In fact, Iraq War veteran Tammy Duckworth, who lost both legs in combat, won a seat in the US Congress in 2012; revulsion to her injuries was never an issue in this most public forum.

A third argument in support of the combat exclusion policy is that of reduced readiness. Specifically, some say that rampant fraternization will occur if women are allowed in combat units, because male commanders will show favoritism to female soldiers for sexual favors, thus causing resentment among male soldiers and leading to reduced unit morale and cohesion. This could be true. One must then ask why these issues would be any more acute in combat formations than they are in noncombat units, where women are already integrated. If anything, the higher risk of death or injury in combat units may reduce the likelihood of these distractions as the mind is focused by heightened risk in a combat mission. Another aspect of this argument relates to feminine hygiene, health, and pregnancy problems. These concerns are legitimate and real but are no more acute than they are for women serving in noncombat roles. Finally, there's the issue of the physical limitations of women compared to men. There is little question that women generally have less upper body strength and lower stamina than men. There is also no question that *some* women have the requisite upper body strength, stamina, and aggressiveness to succeed in the combat arms. Should all women be barred from the combat arms because many do not have these attributes? Are the combat arms less capable and less ready because all women are excluded based solely on their gender?

Those who advocate for the elimination of the combat exclusion rule offer four general arguments. The first one is that it is unconstitutional to ban all women from the majority of combat positions, as it treats them as an undifferentiated class; some women are qualified and willing to serve in combat positions. Thus, proponents for change argue, women are discriminated against. If challenged in court, the government would have to prove a legitimate and exceedingly pervasive justification for the discriminatory legislation and would have to demonstrate a direct, substantiated relationship between the classifications and critical objectives of the government served by the combat exclusion rule. The burden of proof would be on the government, and the success of women in expanded combat roles in aviation and naval operations would bolster the plaintiffs' case, although courts have historically deferred to the experts on defense and national security matters. The combat exclusion policy will be tested in court, as four servicewomen filed suit in federal court in November of 2012. They claim that the policy is unconstitutional, hurts their careers, and impairs their ability to claim combat injuries with the VA.

A second argument for eliminating the combat exclusion policy is that it denies women, consciously or unconsciously, the claim to the full range of citizenship rights in a way similar to denying women the right to vote. Furthermore, it places an unfair burden on men to carry the combat load when women are qualified and willing. Advocates of women in combat argue that when women take on greater responsibilities as a class it enhances and justifies their claims to rights.

Third, advocates for change argue that combat exclusion adversely affects career advancement for women in the military, creating a "brass ceiling," since service in combat is generally a key to selection to higher ranks. The US Supreme Court has ruled in Schlesenger v. Ballard that combat exclusion adversely affects the advancement of women in the military. Although promotion rates for women in the military are improving, they are still absent proportionately in the highest ranks. Finally, limited opportunity to reach the highest ranks may cause highly qualified women to leave the military for other careers with greater opportunities; there are Fortune 500 companies headed by women but no female members of the Joint Chiefs of Staff.

The fourth argument, to which I have already alluded, is that the US military is less capable and less ready as a result of the combat exclusion policy. The effect is most acute in the army and Marine Corps, where the largest proportion of excluded positions and military occupation specialties exist, because at the margins, less qualified men are serving because more qualified women are excluded as a class. *All* women are excluded because *many* are not qualified.

As troubling and challenging as the combat exclusion policy may be to the current and future success of the AVF, sexual violence against women may be an even greater issue. The combat exclusion issue is one of omission, which is largely defended by policy and to a lesser extent by culture. Sexual violence is an issue of commission that is influenced by culture and has been largely immune to changes in policy and sanctimonious pronouncements of zero tolerance by the Pentagon and Congress and concerns expressed by various nongovernmental organizations and victims.

Most Americans are periodically reminded that there is a problem regarding sexual violence in the military by high-profile events that make headlines; several stand out. In 1991, more than one hundred United States Navy and Marine Corps aviation officers were alleged to have sexually assaulted eighty-three women and seven men at the thirty-fifth Annual Tailhook Association Symposium in Las Vegas, Nevada. The navy's initial investigation was viewed as a whitewash, and a second investigation resulted in a number of officers being disciplined or reprimanded including several admirals. There was also a backlash to the findings and consequences to individual officers in the navy imposed by serving and retired aviators and some high-level government officials. The incident and investigations resulted in no substantive policy or regulation changes to reduce sexual harassment and sexual violence in the military. In 1995, the army brought charges against twelve male commissioned and noncommissioned officers at Aberdeen Proving Ground in Maryland for sexual assault of female trainees under their command. Among the charges brought against the twelve were rape, sodomy, adultery, communicating a threat, and obstructing justice. The army's response was to establish a hotline to report sexual harassment. In January 2003, an anonymous e-mail was sent to the secretary of the air force and the air force chief of staff, several members of Congress, and some media representatives, stating that sexual assault was rampant at the United States Air Force Academy and that the problem was being ignored by the academy leadership. Several investigations and working groups were initiated by the secretary of the air force, resulting in a report in September 2004. The report stated that 12 percent of the women in the academy's 2003 graduating class were victims of rape or attempted rape and that 70 percent of the women enrolled at the time alleged that they had been subjected to sexual harassment. Twenty-two percent said that they had been pressured for sexual favors. Most victims were freshmen or sophomores under twenty-one years of age. There is reason to believe that the leadership was aware of the problem but did little to address it. The 2004 report was met by a professed commitment to zero tolerance, and a new leadership was installed at the academy. Beyond this, there were few changes, and no substantive discipline of senior leaders was imposed. In fact, in 2005 the acting secretary of the air force, Peter B. Teets, wrote that former commanders and other air force officers should not be prosecuted because they "acted in good faith" and "were not intentionally or willfully derelict in their duties" as they attempted to deal with the academy's sexual assault problem[17]. It is reasonable to assume that some of the rape victims and their parents would disagree.

In November of 2012, the air force released its report on sexual abuse of recruits at Lackland Air Force Base in Texas where recruits undergo basic training. Investigations of twenty-five military trainers have resulted in charges against eleven, and five have already been convicted of charges ranging from rape to inappropriate relations with recruits. In addition, two commanding officers have been removed and six others have received disciplinary action. This is the same air force that stated that it had zero tolerance for sexual violence in response to the Air Force Academy scandal in 2004.

As troubling, frustrating, and embarrassing as these four high-visibility scandals may be to the American people, the Pentagon, or Congress, they pale in comparison to the less visible routine of sexual violence that occurs every day in the US military. Sexual violence has become so routine that the military has officially termed rape, sexual violence, and sexual harassment *military sexual trauma*, an Orwellian designation that masks violent crime and focuses on the victims (out of respect for victims, I decline to use this term).

The facts and figures regarding this daily occurrence of sexual violence as reported by the DOD are stunning:

- In fiscal year 2011, 3,192 military sexual assaults were reported; this represented a 1 percent increase from fiscal year 2012.
- Sexual assaults are generally underreported and more so in military settings due to the command structure and investigation and adjudication procedures. The DOD estimates that of the

---

[17] "No punishment recommended in sexual assault scandal" http://rockymoutain news.com/drmn/state/article/0,1299,DRMN. *Rocky Mountain News*. 26 March 2005. Retrieved 28 March 2005.

19,000 sexual assaults that occurred in 2010, only 13.5 percent of the victims reported the assaults. In May of 2013, the Pentagon reported that there were 26,000 sexual assaults in 2012, a 37 percent increase over 2011.

- Approximately 55 percent of women and 38 percent of men who reported sexual assault in 2012 reported that their assailant sexually harassed or stalked them prior to the rape or sexual assault.

- Of the 3,192 sexual assaults reported in 2011, 1,518 were considered actionable by the military, a 22 percent decrease from 2010. Prosecution rates for sexual violence in the military are low. Fewer than 8 percent of reported cases went to trial; 191 resulted in conviction. Of those convicted, 148 served jail sentences. Remarkably, an estimated 10 percent of the perpetrators were allowed to resign in lieu of court martial. The military allowed accused rapists to resign from the military in order to avoid trial.

- One out of three convicted sex offenders remain in the military, where there is no military sex offender registry. Currently only the navy and Air Force discharge all convicted sex offenders either through punitive discharge or administrative separation. Legislation has been introduced in both the House and Senate that requires the dismissal or dishonorable discharge of any service member found guilty of rape, sexual assault, forcible sodomy, or an attempt to commit any of those offenses.

- Another aspect of sexual violence in the military is that it is even more difficult to prosecute the alleged offender than it is in the civilian system. The victim's trauma, victim baiting, lack of evidence, and the scarcity of witnesses make prosecution difficult. Rape victims in the military judicial system are at the mercy of the judgment of local commanders, a bias to protecting the institution, and an authoritarian, male-dominated structure. Victims have no appeal procedure as in the civil system because of a broad interpretation of the Feres doctrine resulting from the 1950 Supreme Court decision in Feres vs. United States, which effectively provides that rape in the military is "incident to service." I will leave it to the reader to judge the wisdom of this interpretation and whether carving out an exception to the doctrine in cases of rape makes sense. For now, rape is "incident to service" in our all-volunteer military.

The effects of the pervasive and long-standing sexual violence against women on the AVF in terms of recruiting, retention, and readiness are significant. Sexual violence is the leading cause of PTSD among women veterans. Rape, sexual assault, and sexual harassment are also risk factors for homelessness among women veterans. In fiscal year 2010, 39 to 53 percent of Veterans Health Administration users who were victims of sexual violence in the military were homeless compared to 22 percent of all Veterans Health Administration users. Rape, sexual assault, and sexual harassment survivors have a high rate of substance abuse and difficulty finding employment after military discharge as a result of depression, stress, and other mental and emotional health issues resulting from their experience.

The cost of the crisis is not limited to the victims and their families. The already overburdened Veterans Administration (VA) in 2009 had more than sixty-five thousand cases of sexual violence outpatient care; 59.6 percent of these were women 40.4 percent men. The VA spent approximately $10,880 on health care per military sexual assault survivor. This means that in the midst of a fiscal crisis in the United States, in 2010 the VA spent millions of taxpayer dollars to treat sexual-assault victims. Additionally, DOD estimates that in 2010 its legal expenses from sexual assault cases were more than $19 million.

In summarizing the role of women in the AVF, it is clear that they have made a major contribution to making it work. Their contribution to the force has risen from less than 2 percent in 1973 to more than 14 percent today. Given the fact that women make up almost 50 percent of the population, one could argue that they are still underrepresented and that the effect of this underrepresentation has a greater impact on the quality of our force than the quantity. How many highly qualified women decline to enter military service or decline to reenlist because they are discriminated against as a result of the combat exclusion policy? How many make similar decisions because of the military's history of sexual violence and its failure to stop it? Is the AVF working for women today, and will it work in the future?

Before moving to a conclusion of this book and engaging the question of whether the AVF is working and whether it will work in the future, it may be helpful to discuss three issues. First, what are the links or relationships between the policies employed over the past decade to man and deploy the force and critical issues facing the military today? Second, what are some of the issues facing the military recruiting commands in the foreseeable future? Is recruiting high quality enlistees likely to become more or less challenging? Third, what are the most likely war-fighting requirements of the United States in the foreseeable future—who are we likely to fight, how good are they, and what might be required? This is relevant to those who might argue that questions about the AVF are moot since the United States will never again go to war.

Cause and Effect (or Contribution)

To this point I have identified a list of policy measures on the part of the military to support the AVF, especially over the past ten years when it has been most severely tested. Among them are the following:

- stop-loss
- unprecedented use of enlistment and reenlistment bonuses
- unprecedented use of prescription psychotropic drugs
- consciously ignoring physical fitness and weight control failures prior to deployments, particularly for National Guard and reserve members
- use of contractors to perform functions traditionally reserved to the uniformed military

- unprecedented use of the National Guard and reserve to fight sustained wars, prompting it to become an operational rather than a strategic reserve
- multiple deployments with dwell times cut in half, clearly violating DOD policy
- the dramatic increase in the participation of women in the military from 2 percent of the force in 1973 to almost 15 percent today
- lowered enlistment standards for age, education, physical fitness, and criminal history
- enhanced incentives to motivate noncitizens to enlist, particularly in medical and language specialties

In addition to these policy decisions that allowed the AVF to survive the past twelve years of war, the AVF was helped immensely by the 1989 collapse of the Soviet Union, which allowed the United States to reduce the size of its force. Fewer people were required to serve; fewer people were required to be recruited. The peace dividend paid off as long as peace lasted. In 2002 it may have seemed more like a peace penalty to those responsible for the AVF. The military struggled not only to man the force but also to provide forces in the war zone. The Cold War's effect on the AVF was structural. Variations in the civilian unemployment rate, youth obesity, high-school dropout rates, and the propensity to serve, on the other hand, are issues that Pentagon force planners will have to project and react to as long as we have a military.

CHAPTER 5 – EFFECTS OF SAVING THE ALL-VOLUNTEER FORCE

How the global war on terror breaks not the force, but volunteers and families.

P olicies intended to support the AVF may have caused some of the most troubling issues that our military faces today. In some cases, *cause* may be too strong a term; *contribution* may be more appropriate. I am not asserting that these effects would all disappear if we did not have an all-volunteer force. Fear, apathy, ignorance, and guilt might cause us to ignore, minimize, or rationalize these effects or assign their resolution to others who patronize the general public with catch phrases like "zero tolerance" and "heroic sacrifice." But the effects still do exist. Among the effects to be considered are the following:

Suicide

Virtually all observers of US military affairs agree that there is deep concern over the issue of suicide not only in the active force but also among veterans. Members of Congress, senior military members, veterans groups, and military families have all expressed concern. Not surprisingly, the general public is not well informed or particularly concerned. At the end of 2012, the DOD reported that 482 service members committed suicide compared to 310 who died in combat during the year. In 2011 there were 301 suicides. The increase occurred despite initiatives by the DOD to stop the rising number of suicides. Until 2008, the suicide rate for the active military was far below that of the general population, and the current rate of suicide in the military is three times what it was in 2001 after doubling between 2001 and 2006. As tragic as the suicide rate in the military is, it is even more tragic—or perhaps ironic—that combat deaths are used as the measure of comparison. What does this tell us about the current state of the AVF?

The story of suicides among veterans is even more alarming. While the government does not keep an official record of veteran suicides, the VA in 2010 said that veterans account for approximately 20 percent of the estimated thirty thousand suicides committed in the United States each year. The *Army Times* reported in 2010 that an average of eighteen US military veterans take their own lives each day. One study by the epidemiology and biostatistics department at the University of Georgia found that veterans were twice as likely to commit suicide as nonveterans and that veterans aged twenty to twenty-four were two to four times more likely to commit suicide than their nonveteran peers. There may be some argument about specific data and reporting, but there is no debate about the severity of the military's suicide crisis or its direction.

Bending the suicide rate curve down is difficult. One of the major problems to overcome is the stigma of asking for help in a macho military environment where doing so is often seen as a sign of weakness. Another issue is the availability of resources to those in need of help, particularly veterans in rural areas. In some cases drug and alcohol abuse problems must be dealt with to get at the root causes. Finally, some people just don't get it. **In early 2012, Major General Dana Pittard, commander of the First Armored Division and Fort Bliss, Texas, stated, " I have now come to the conclusion that suicide is an absolutely selfish act. I am personally fed up with soldiers who** are choosing to take their own lives so that others can clean up the mess. Be an adult, act like an adult, and deal with your real life problems like the rest of us."[18] He later retracted but did not apologize for the statement. His remarks drew a public rebuke from the army, but he remained in command.

Post-Traumatic Stress Disorder

PTSD is an anxiety disorder that can occur after an individual has been through a traumatic event, such as combat. It is the signature injury (along with traumatic brain injury) of the wars in Iraq and Afghanistan. PTSD is not new or unique to these wars and has been apparent in previous wars, often under the name of combat stress, combat fatigue, or various forms of nervous breakdown. Several factors make PTSD more prevalent in these wars. First is the nature of the wars. Counterinsurgency offers a 360 degree front for the individual service member, requiring constant vigilance while integrating with an indigenous population. Second is improved body armor, which protects combatants' vital organs from physical injury that in previous wars might have removed them from the battlefield but does not protect them from the mental and psychological injury of staying in the fight longer. This reduction of physical wounds leads to a higher probability of receiving the "invisible wounds" of PTSD. A third factor driving PTSD severity in these wars is the policy of repeat deployment with reduced dwell time outside the war zones to recover and decompress. Although the DOD, the VA, and the RAND Corporation continue to study the relationship between occurrence of PTSD and multiple deployments, studies already completed indicate that a second or third deployment to Iraq or Afghanistan nearly doubles the probability of PTSD for the redeployed service member.

PTSD manifests itself in physical, behavioral, and psychological ways: attention deficit, listlessness, mood swings, anxiety, and depression

---

18 "Suicides Among US Troops Averaging One a Day in 2012," *USA Today*, Rafiq Maqbool, June 7, 2012.

often lead to alcohol and drug abuse, criminal behavior, domestic violence, unemployment, homelessness, and suicide. Families and communities suffer and bear the cost along with the service member or veteran. Cases of PTSD vary in severity and the time it takes for treatment to have an effect, the likelihood that a victim will seek and continue treatment, and the time it takes for symptoms to manifest themselves (which may be years in some cases). Given all these variables, there is no definitive proportion of service members who suffer from PTSD or seek treatment. Estimates of the percentage of veterans of Iraq and Afghanistan who suffer from PTSD range from 20 to 30 percent, and only about 50 percent will get the treatment they need, either because of their own failure or the failure of the DOD or VA medical systems.

PTSD is a very difficult medical issue to deal with. It is also a complex political and strategic issue in the Pentagon and Congress that could generate uncomfortable questions regarding the war and the AVF. The DOD and the VA have taken strong measures to deal with the issue. Nonetheless, again, people just don't get it. On May 17, 2012, the *New York Times* reported on a problem with the military's disability evaluation system, which determines whether injured soldiers are fit to remain in the military. The report stated,

> Concerns about the system emerged last fall after soldiers at Joint Base Lewis-McCord in Tacoma told Senator Patty Murry, a Democrat of Washington, that their diagnosis of post-traumatic stress disorder had been changed by doctors at Madigan Army Medical Center to lesser conditions. The soldiers asserted that the changes were done to save the Army money.
>
> That complaint seemed to gain credibility with the emergence of an internal Army memorandum in February that quoted a Madigan doctor saying that Army clinicians needed to be "good stewards" of taxpayer dollars and that a PTSD diagnosis could cost $1.5 million in disability compensation over a soldier's lifetime.

Congressional inquiries and army investigations were immediately initiated, resulting in more than one hundred of the three hundred PTSD diagnoses being reinstated. And the DOD initiated a system-wide analysis at the army level. Nonetheless, damage was done in that trust in the system suffered and psychologically wounded soldiers were made to suffer even more at the hands of a misguided bureaucracy that was consciously or unconsciously protecting a method of manning our forces.

Homelessness

For any nation, having a significant segment of its population homeless is a problem. For developed nations it is an embarrassment. When a large portion of those homeless also are veterans of the nation's military, it is a tragedy. The secretary of the Veterans Affairs Administration, General Eric Shinseki, said, "those who have served its nation as veterans should never find themselves on the street, living without care and without hope."[19] The unfortunate reality, though, is that America has large numbers of homeless veterans.

Veterans represent approximately 25 percent of the homeless people in the United States though they represent less than 10 percent of the general adult population. According to the National Coalition for the Homeless, between 130,000 and 200,000 veterans are homeless on any given night. Other studies have estimated an even higher portion of the homeless to be veterans. The coalition also estimates that 400,000 veterans will experience homelessness during the course of a year..

As alarming as these figures are, there is a strong possibility that they may rise, since homelessness among veterans is a secondary effect of causes such as PTSD, traumatic brain injury, prescription and illegal drug abuse, alcohol abuse, crime, depression, and frayed family and social relationships resulting from long and repeated deployments.

---

19 Statement made at the "VA National Summit Ending Homelessness Among Veterans" on Nov. 3, 2009 and reported on the official website of the U.S. Air Force on Nov. 4, 2009

Homelessness is also influenced by economic conditions and unemployment. The disproportionately high homelessness rate among veterans is also influenced by the fact that our service members are recruited primarily from the third and fourth socioeconomic quintiles of the nation, where the social and financial safety net is weakest. Those in this group often lack the skill sets and resources to deal with the administrative and bureaucratic hurdles between them and help. Finally, government budget deficits and debt may make it more difficult to secure the funding increases to the VA and other community services to deal effectively with the problem. An increase in PTSD and other medical conditions that drive homelessness, unemployment, a weak social support net for veterans, and budget pressures do not bode well for fixing the homeless veteran issue soon.

The leader of the Veterans Administration, Gen. Eric Shinseki, is acutely aware of the issue and stated in 2009 that "President Obama and I are personally committed to ending homelessness among veterans within the next five years." That commitment is unlikely to be fulfilled. His initiatives include the Post-9/11 GI Bill; collaborating with the Small Business Administration to create veteran-owned businesses; spending more than $500 million on specific homeless programs; aggressive programs to diagnose and treat the physical, mental, and emotional conditions that lead to homelessness; and partnering with 600 community organizations and 240 public housing authorities. Because of increasing backlogs at the VA, staffing shortfalls, and large numbers of service members being discharged from active duty, these initiatives have, at best, stabilized the problem.

We gratuitously refer to service members and military veterans as heroes. A skeptical and informed observer of American civil-military affairs might ask, "Why does America tolerate 200,000 homeless heroes?"

Veteran Unemployment

Unemployment is a serious problem in the United States. It is not only an economic problem but also, and perhaps more importantly, a social problem that tears at the fabric of our national identity as it challenges the concept of the land of opportunity. At the individual level it strikes at a person's dignity, particularly for the long-term unemployed. For veterans the problem is greater than for nonveterans. President Obama, in a speech in Dallas in late 2011, said, "Think about it. We ask these men and women to leave their families, disrupt their career, risk their lives for our nation. The last thing they should have to do is fight for a job when they come home."

Notwithstanding the president's comment, that is exactly what they have to do. And they are losing the fight. In 2012, the unemployment rate for Iraq and Afghanistan veterans was 9.9 percent, down from 12.1 percent in 2011. The national average, though, was 7.8 percent. About 205,000 Iraq and Afghanistan veterans were unemployed. Some segments of the veteran population are particularly hard hit. In 2011, at what appeared to be the height of the problem, unemployment among veterans in the eighteen- to twenty-four-year-old age group was 33.2 percent compared 14.9 percent among their nonveteran peers. Also in 2011, unemployment among women veterans who had served since 2001 was 16.8 percent compared to 7.8 percent for nonveteran women.[20] Unemployment statistics are among the most suspect and questioned among all those issued by the government, but few question whether veterans who have served since 2001 are more likely to be unemployed than their nonveteran counterparts. In March of 2012, the *Huffington Post* cited a quote regarding veteran unemployment from Kevin Schmiegel, vice-president of the US Chamber of Commerce's veteran-employment programs: "This is a national security issue. What happens to the all volunteer force? We're not going to be able to recruit enough people to serve in the military if we don't do something now." Schmiegal's observation is informed by the fact that a large part of the marketing pitch to potential military recruits is that the military prepares service members for the civilian working world while the data challenge that pitch.

---

[20] "Jobless Rates for Young and Female Vets Climb in Late 2011," *USA Today*, Gregg Zoreya, January 6, 2012.

There are a number of explanations offered why young veterans are 20 to 30 percent more likely to be unemployed than their nonveteran peers. First is that they were likely to have been unemployed or underemployed before enlisting; that's why they enlisted. And they may have come from economically depressed areas that are no less (or perhaps more) depressed when they return after their discharge. Second, veterans have difficulty describing and communicating skill sets learned in the military to civilian hiring managers. Part of this problem is that most of the hiring managers never served in the military, and many skill sets, such as that of an armor crewman, scout, or explosive ordinance disposal specialist, don't have direct civilian applications. Third, with medical costs rising rapidly for most civilian employers, many are reluctant to take on the additional risks of invisible injuries (PTSD and TBI) or long-term spine, back, and knee effects of combat. Fourth, for reservists and National Guardsmen, as I noted earlier, the prospect of repeat deployments that require the employer to replace the service member while deployed and then reinstate him or her upon return is a deterrent, particularly for small businesses. Finally, many city, county, and state governments are budget constrained, thus reducing work forces where veterans have historically enjoyed a hiring preference. Female veterans may be most acutely affected by this development.

Programs are in place and more are emerging to address the problem of veteran unemployment. The federal government, primarily through the Veterans Administration (and the Labor Department and the Small Business Administration) has reinforced a number of established programs and recently introduced new initiatives. Civic organizations have also pitched in with programs like Operation: Hire Our Heroes and well-publicized job fairs for veterans and businesses. Veterans organizations including the Iraq and Afghanistan Veterans Association have also been active in addressing the problem. Finally, some businesses have joined the effort. In January 2013, Walmart committed to hire 100,000 veterans in the next five years (I should note that Walmart's president and chief executive, William S. Simon, is a navy veteran). Despite these initiatives and a host of others, veteran unemployment remains consistently higher than that of nonveterans. Many observers fear that ending the Afghan war, downsizing the army (from 560,000 soldiers to 490,000), and the delayed emergence of PTSD cases will cause veteran unemployment to remain well above that of nonveterans, a sad prospect for "heroes."

Drug Abuse

Drug and alcohol abuse has historically been of concern to the military because of its adverse impact on the discipline and physical and mental fitness of its troops. Until the early part of this century, the military's drug problem centered on illegal street drugs and occasional abuses of some rarely prescribed drugs. All that changed decisively as the military reversed its policy regarding the prescription of psychotropic drugs to deal with stress, anxiety, depression, sleep disorders, anger, paranoia, and suicide among its members. The policy change was made in order to preserve the fighting strength of a stretched volunteer force. Drugs were substituted for counselors, psychologists, and psychiatrists, who were in short supply in the military medical system. At this time we have no way of knowing what the medium- or long-term effects of the unprecedented prescription of these drugs will have on those service members to whom they were prescribed. As I outlined earlier in this book, a significant minority of those fighting in Iraq and Afghanistan were issued psychotropic drugs by military health professionals. Often drugs were prescribed off label. Often more than one drug was prescribed, creating a drug cocktail. In many cases the drugs are likely to be addictive.

It would require hope or magical thinking to believe that all of these service members could be effectively and permanently weaned off these drugs. The military medical system and the VA are overwhelmed (I will address the VA system later) and lack sufficient health care professionals. Community health-care systems have similar staffing issues and in many cases are budget constrained. A final piece of this equation is the reluctance of many veterans and service members to seek medical treatment and the difficulty some have in transporting themselves to distant treatment facilities.

This is an issue that affects the service member or veteran physically and mentally. It also impacts veteran unemployment and veterans' ability to reintegrate into civilian society. Families are also affected as they try to help the service member or veteran while dealing with the effects of domestic violence, child abuse, divorce, and suicide. These consequences are not unique to prescription drug abuse in the military; our society as a whole experiences them every day. What is unique is the unintended social consequence of creating thousands of drug-related problems in order to preserve the fighting strength of a stretched all-volunteer force.

Domestic Violence and Family Abuse

An aspect of the military that is invisible to much of the American public is the strain placed on military families; this invisibility is understandable given that most people have never served. Frequent relocations, long separations for training, financial stress for young families, separation from traditional family support networks, and difficulties for a spouse to gain employment or pursue a career are long-standing realities of military life. Since 2001 we have added the stress of repeated long combat deployments with little dwell time, PTSD, TBI, effects of prescription drugs, and the increased prospect of serious physical harm or death to these traditional stressors on military families. Although one might counter that they volunteered, the effects are sobering, far reaching, and intergenerational.

There are a number of data points that inform the occurrence of domestic violence and stress in the military as noted in the US Army's 2012 report *Generating Health and Discipline in the Force Ahead of the Strategic Reset*:

- From 2000 to 2009, the number of duty years lost as a result of hospitalization for behavioral health disorders among active-duty service members increased 300 percent.

- A male soldier with PTSD is 1.9 to 3.1 times more likely to demonstrate aggression toward his female partner than a soldier not suffering from PTSD.
- In 2001 there were 2,771 convictions for family abuse cases in the army. The report further states that "Family abuse may be an underreported offense due to the fact that law enforcement often categorizes incidence of family abuse under a variety of other assault related charges." Underreporting may also result from cases being discharged through administrative actions and nonjudicial punishment.
- From 2006 to 2011, family abuse offenses increased 61 percent and offenders increased 56 percent.
- From 2001 to 2011, substantiated crimes of domestic violence increased 85 percent, and substantiated crimes of child abuse increased 44 percent.
- Referrals to the army's family advocacy program, an initiative to assist struggling families, increased from 2008 to 2011 by 50 percent for domestic violence and 62 percent for child abuse. Unfortunately, only 91 percent of those referred for domestic violence and 93 percent of those referred for child abuse enrolled. More alarming, only 60 percent and 63 percent respectively completed the program. This may help to explain the recidivism rate for active-duty soldiers for domestic violence, which rose from 8 percent in 2001 to more than 12 percent in 2011 at the same installations in the same year.
- Finally, alcohol use associated with substantiated domestic violence and child abuse increased 54 percent and 40 percent respectively from 2001 to 2011.

The strain placed on the AVF and the families that man it are clearly reflected in the data. Measures taken to man the force and deploy sufficient troop strength have clearly contributed to the increase in domestic violence and child abuse in the military in the 2001–2011 time frame in which we have rigorously tested the all-volunteer concept.

If we saw the same dramatic increases in society as a whole, it would be considered a crisis. This crisis is confined to those who have skin in the game. The fact that thirty thousand service members were divorced in 2011 is not surprising. This was the highest number of military divorces since 1999. Military divorces are particularly troublesome because of the different states and jurisdictions in which the two parties may reside due to the normal cycle of military transfer. For the same reason, military divorces are even more tragic when children are involved, as custody disputes and visitation arrangements are more complex.

Even without instances of domestic violence and child abuse, evidence of stress on military families is well documented. A study conducted by the Defense Manpower Data Center reported the following survey results:

- From 2006 to 2010, the number of army spouses experiencing stress rose from 46 percent to 56 percent.
- Forty-four percent reported concerns about finances, with only 34 percent reporting that they had more than $500 in savings.
- Of the 54 percent of army spouses who were working or looking for work (that is, in the labor pool), 29 percent were unemployed.
- Nineteen percent of those surveyed stated that they were in counseling, with the majority receiving counseling for stress, family, and marital issues.

The stress level of children in military families is also high due to frequent relocations, frequent separations from parents while they are deployed or training, and the trauma of the potential or reality of a parent's combat death or severe physical or mental injury. Children are also affected by the high stress level of the nondeployed parent. Sociologists insist on confirming the obvious; a 2011 study reported in *Science Daily* found that children of service members deployed in Iraq or Afghanistan for long periods are more likely to suffer from behavioral health issues than children whose parents are not deployed. Among the 6,579 mental health diagnoses observed in these children of deployed parents, acute stress reaction and adjustment disorders, depressive disorders, and behavioral disorders were most frequent. It is reasonable to assume that these issues make academic progress in school more difficult, thus affecting the future professional and academic success of these children—an intergenerational impact that awaits us.

A second intergenerational impact is thrust upon grandparents who become temporary full-time care givers to grandchildren when single parents are deployed or when both parents are simultaneously deployed. The stress of caring for young children in one's later years after having become accustomed to a slower pace of life can be daunting. Parents, grandparents, and spouses are also often called upon to be caregivers to seriously injured or disabled veterans who are suffering from PTSD, TBI, drug addiction, amputation, or other serious injuries that require long-term, around-the-clock care. The care provided comes at the expense of the caregiver financially, professionally, and emotionally. Improved body armor and greatly improved battlefield medicine have reduced the number of wounded who would otherwise have died in combat but have delivered a large number of physically and psychologically wounded soldiers into the arms of a small, caring portion of our nation who have skin in the game.

Veterans Administration Backlog

Long, repeated deployments to war zones and the unprecedented prescription of psychotropic drugs and painkillers have had a negative effect on the physical, emotional, and psychological health of the force. The military medical system and the Veterans Administration initially responded well to the increased demands for their services. In fact, some aspects of military medicine were groundbreaking and cutting-edge and informed civilian practice, including new ways of treating bullet wounds, severe burns, and polytrauma and improvements in speedy evacuations and prosthetics. The combination of improved body armor and advanced medical practices has saved the lives of many who would have died in previous wars. Many survivors were unable to continue their military careers and were discharged but still required a significant amount of medical care, which is the function of the Veterans Administration.

It is not the purpose of this book to describe the issues faced by the VA, judge its leadership, or identify and evaluate the steps it has taken to improve its performance. But members of Congress have looked closely at these issues and requested the General Accounting Office (GAO) to report on its performance. In December 2012 the GAO reported the following:

- The VA backlog has tripled since 2009.
- The average length of time it took to complete a claim rose from 161 days in 2009 to 260 in 2012. Here is the average number of days it took to complete a claim by year:

	2009	2010	2011	2012
Pending:	116	117	198	254
Complete:	161	166	188	260

- While the Veterans Benefits Administration's stated goal is to process all claims within 125 days by fiscal year 2015, it has declined to provide Congress with interim benchmarks.
- The timeliness of appeals processing has decreased 56 percent at VA regional offices over the past several years.
- Notices of Disagreement by veterans of benefit determinations by the VA are also backlogged. Time spent waiting for decisions has nearly doubled:

	2009	2010	2011	2012
Cases Received:	124,000	141,000	116,000	122,000
Awaiting Decision:	92,000	116,000	150,000	163,000

A reputable veterans organization, VAwatchdog.org, reported on January 24, 2013, that as of January 19, 2013, there were 902,402 claims pending and 69.4 percent of all claims were backlogged. Every one of these 902,402 claims was made by one of the "heroes" we refer to in other contexts. They volunteered for military service not bureaucratic failure.

The failure of the VA system to effectively process claims of benefits and service has a subtle and real impact on the AVF. It violates service members' trust that they and their families will be taken care of in a timely manner. Conditions that generate the claims are not getting any better while the claims are backlogged. The VA's failure also impacts recruiting and retention in the AVF. Is an individual more or less likely to enlist or reenlist knowing that the system to take care of them in the event of injury is failing? Statements about process improvements, increased staffing, and deep concern by the VA do not negate hard data or counteract the effects of this failure on the AVF.

Nobel Prize–winning economist Dr. Joseph Stinglitz and his co-author Linda Bilmes put the VA's performance in perspective in their 2008 book *The Three Trillion Dollar War.* They write,

> The VBA takes an average of six months to process an original claim, and an average of nearly two years to process an appeal. By contrast, the private sector health care/financial services industry processes over 25 billion claims a year, with 98% processed within sixty days of receiving the claim, including the time required for claims that are disputed. Perhaps the most distressing implication of the six month long bottleneck in the VA claims process is that it deprives veterans of benefits at the precise moment when—particularly for those in a state of mental distress—they are most at risk of suicide, falling into substance abuse, divorce, losing their job, or becoming homeless.

Reduced Trust in the Military

Measures taken to support the AVF directly or indirectly, particularly since the attacks of 9/11, have in many cases called the judgment and integrity of the military into question. Questions have been raised at the policy level by government officials, the media, and the general public, with mixed results. The population that has been more directly affected by these measures—those who serve—is precluded from speaking out; but some opt out by not reenlisting or decline to join in the first place.

At the strategic level, we were told that the invasion of Iraq would be quick and inexpensive and that we would be greeted as liberators. Thus the invasion would require a small number of troops for a short period of time that the AVF could easily support. Iraqis did not receive that memo, and the invasion fostered sectarian violence that morphed into mass insurgency bordering on civil war. In 2002 we were told that these were "dead enders" who would quickly be subdued, another memo the other parties apparently did not receive. We then settled into a long armed occupation with an all-volunteer force too small to meet the requirements without changing policies.

Among the policy changes employed to support the AVF concept, stop-loss was perhaps the most visible. More than 120,000 soldiers have had their active-duty service involuntarily extended by stop-loss orders. The policy, although technically legal, was seen by many, including members of Congress and the general public, as a backdoor draft totally inconsistent with the all-volunteer concept of manning the force. Stop-loss affected only a small segment of the already small slice of the American population who served. But the message to them and those who might consider enlisting did not strengthen their trust in the military. The military further undercut its own integrity by choosing to suspend the discharge of service members under the provisions of Don't Ask Don't Tell. At the same time that the Pentagon was defending DADT because the open service of gays and lesbians supposedly would adversely affect morale, cohesion, and discipline, it was knowingly sending gay and lesbian service members into harm's way. Logic and ethical judgment were sacrificed to support the AVF.

Conscious decisions to decrease dwell time and increase the length of combat tours despite knowing the effect they would have on the emotional and psychological health of the force also reduced trust. Rationalizing the likely adverse effects on service members with a stoic call to duty does not mitigate the predictable effects. This trade-off and its ongoing effects on the trust between soldiers and the institutional army are tragically obvious in the decision to employ prescription drugs to preserve the fighting strength of the force.

A further breach of trust with the American people—and, more importantly, with those serving and their families—occurred when the Pentagon decided to lower its accession standards for new recruits beginning in 2005. Previously the military had touted its high standards, but when recruiting shortfalls surfaced, the standards for age, education, physical fitness, and moral rectitude were cast aside. Standards were sacrificed to preserve the all-volunteer concept, and those already serving were expected to ignore the hypocrisy and compensate for its consequences.

Finally, many viewed the repeat deployments of thousands of National Guard and reserve service members as a violation of the intent and purpose of reserve forces. It is true that some in these units saw their involvement as an affirmation of their professionalism and patriotism, but many saw it as a perversion of their contract. The latter group enlisted in the strategic reserves, which morphed into operational reserves to support the all-volunteer concept. As a result, many who joined or might have joined the strategic reserve either left or never enlisted. This change will have a lasting impact on the ability of the reserve components to recruit and retain high-quality service members.

Policies that have been outlined here have caused or contributed to the effects listed below. These effects have been visited upon not only service members and their families but also the nation as a whole and the military as an institution:

- suicide
- PTSD

- veteran homelessness
- domestic violence
- divorce
- reduced trust in the military
- VA backlog
- national debt
- impaired military capabilities
- the underrepresentation in the military of the first socioeconomic quintile

These causes (or contributors) and effects may be effectively depicted in the matrix below, which shows where they might merge. I do not suggest that any policy decision is the sole cause of any of the effects, but each does, at a minimum, contribute to these issues. Are we willing to fight the next war while employing the same policies, knowing the effects they have created?

	Suicide	PTSD	Homelessness	Unemployment	Institutional Trust	VA Backlog	National Debt	Domestic Violence	Divorce	Reduced Mil. Capability	Under represent Elite	Drug/Alcohol Abuse
Stop-loss					X							
Bonuses							X				X	
Use of prescription drugs	X	X	X	X		X						X
DADT					X							
APFT Weight Control					X							
Contractors							X			X		
Use of reserve components				X	X	X						
Multiple deployments	X	X	X	X		X		X	X		X	X
Women			X	X	X						X	
Lower standards	X	X	X	X	X					X		
Use of noncitizens					X						X	

The April 16, 2010, testimony of General Eric Shinseki, the secretary of the Veterans Affairs Administration and the former army chief of staff, summarizes the effects of our current policies. General Shinseki was seriously wounded in Vietnam. He said that he was troubled by two images American service members. The first was an image of new recruits who, he said, "outperform all of our expectations—great youngsters." The second image is that of veterans who make up "a disproportionate share of the nation's homeless, jobless, mental health (problems), depressed patients, substance abusers, suicides." He observed that "something happened along the way," and we have to figure out what.

National Debt and the Pentagon Budget

The Gates Commission speculated that the AVF would be affordable. The reality is reflected in a January 2013 report by the Reserve Forces Policy Board, which states that "The fully burdened life cycle cost trends supporting the current All Volunteer force are unsustainable." It further states that "The DoD cost of 'taking care of people' now consumes more than $250 billion or over 50% of the total DoD budget." Personnel costs have grown nearly 90 percent since 2001 for approximately the same size force, according to Secretary of Defense Panetta. Finally, the Center for Strategic and Budgetary Assessment reported in July 2012 that "Over the past decade, the cost per person in the active-duty force increased by 46 percent. If personnel costs continue to grow at that rate and the overall defense budget remains flat with inflation, military personnel cost will consume the entire defense budget by 2039." Accelerating personnel costs and two long wars have produced a rising defense budget. The direct costs of the wars will go away, as we have left Iraq and will exit Afghanistan in 2014. Personnel costs in the AVF will continue to rise and contribute to America's budget deficit and debt for the foreseeable future.

Impaired Military Capabilities

After twelve years of war conducted by a force too small to support dwell time, we have an exhausted force. Over the past ten years, some experts have expressed concern that we would break the force. The force did not break, but thousands of service members and their families have broken. The American ground forces are exhausted, the American people are war weary, and most senior military leaders agree that our army needs to reset itself in terms of personnel and equipment. This recent history and our current state should prompt us to think more deeply about our options regarding Iran and Syria than we did about Iraq and Afghanistan.

Underrepresented First Socioeconomic Quintile

Since the phrase "a rich man's war and a poor man's fight" was first heard during our Civil War, the burdens of war have continued to fall on the lower and middle classes of our nation. Since the Civil War, the substitution and commutation provisions of that era's conscription laws have been rejected. Since 1973, when the AVF came into being, we have provided (unconsciously and without malice) de facto moral cover to a segment of society to opt out of military service. This is a segment whose members enjoy a broader range of options and are likely to occupy positions of power and influence later in life; they will enter those positions absent any military experience. As a result, the civil-military gap I noted earlier will only grow larger.

CHAPTER 6 - THE FUTURE

We will go to war again against capable opponents. Will enough volunteers show up on our side?

R ecruiting high-quality young people in a democracy to serve in a military force has never been an easy task. As outlined earlier in this book, the American experience has been mixed whether conscription was used or not. Success was dependent on a number of factors, most of which are out of the control of the military: perceived threat, propensity to serve, civilian unemployment rates, and patriotic orientation. The Civil War and the Second World War were the only periods in our nation's history when we saw an overwhelming and sustained volunteering for military service driven by the perceived threat to the nation. The only other time we saw such a response was for a few months immediately after the attacks of 9/11. Enlistments soon returned to their normal rates, and within a few years of war we experienced critical recruiting shortfalls.

In assessing the future of manning the force under the all-volunteer concept, we might first look to what policies, practices, and events have worked to sustain the AVF to this point. In the short term, we can expect the force to become somewhat smaller as we withdraw from Afghanistan, thus reducing the requirements for manpower.

Requirements could rise as a result of operations in other areas, such as Iran or North Korea. All of the same policies are available to us in the future: contractors, enlistment and reenlistment bonuses, repeated deployments, stop-loss, overuse of psychotropic drugs, recruitment of noncitizens, unprecedented use of National Guard and reserve forces, and so on. All are available, but at some cost and risk.

The larger climate for recruiting is changing too. General William Wallace, commander of the Army's Training and Doctrine Command, stated in 2006,

> **I have serious thoughts about [the future], and it's got less to do with recruits than ... with the education and fitness of American youth, because all of the trends are going in the wrong direction. Only three out of ten young men and women, ages 17 to 24, are fully qualified to be soldiers. One kid drops out of high school in the United States every 29 seconds—over a million kids dropping out of school. And we have fitness and obesity problems within our youth population, so in an organization like the Army, which values intellect, fitness and morals, and all the trends are going in the wrong direction—that does, indeed, cause me some concern, unless we do something about it.**

In a February 2009 interview with the *Army Times*, Lieutenant General Benjamin Freakley, the army's chief recruiter, amplified General Wallace's concern, noting that "The bottom line is that the army has had to recruit by these lowered standards to maintain a wartime force in one of the most difficult recruiting eras in our history. What we will see in the near future is not a lack of quantity but a potential lack of quality as we access into the army today its leadership for 2040."

It is unlikely that the rates of high-school dropouts and adolescent obesity will improve any time soon. The childhood and adolescent obesity rate nearly tripled in the United States between 1980 and 2000 and in 2008 leveled off at about 32 percent. This is an alarming trend for the nation as a whole and particularly for the military, as the individual physical demands of military operations have not declined over the same period. Similar to obesity, the growing number of young people in the United States diagnosed with asthma will also reduce the pool of potential recruits to the AVF. In 2001, 7 percent of the overall population had asthma. In 2009 it was 8 percent, with rates for children (future recruits) and African Americans even higher than in the rest of the population, according to the American Academy of Asthma and Immunology. Data on the high-school graduation rate is no more encouraging, as the US Department of Education reports that the national average freshman graduation rate for public school students for the class of 2007–2008 was 74.9 percent, a 25.1 percent dropout rate.[21]

What portion of the population is able to meet the physical, mental, and moral standards established to meet the demands of military service? The consensus is about 30 percent and likely to stabilize at this level and perhaps decline slightly in the future. As alarming as this figure is, the number of those willing to serve is even more troublesome. Recruiting success in the future is a function of the percentage of the population that is both willing and able to serve. The DOD is justifiably concerned with the issue of propensity to serve in the military. It is measured in two periodic surveys, the DOD's Youth Poll, a telephone survey of people aged sixteen to twenty-one who have never served in the armed forces, and the University of Michigan's "Monitoring the Future: A Continuing Study of American Youth," which is a questionnaire. Responses to the questions about how likely respondents are to serve in the military are "definitely," "probably," "probably not," and "definitely not." Anyone who responds "definitely" or "probably" is considered to have an "aided propensity to serve." Follow-up studies indicate that the relationship between propensity to serve and actual service is significant. A 2001 study conducted by Orvis and Asch concluded that over half of those who indicated unaided propensity subsequently took the Armed Services Vocational Aptitude Battery (ASVAB) to determine

---

21 US Department of Education, *Trends in High School Dropout and Completion Rates in the United States: 1972–2008.*

their qualification for military occupational specialties, and one-third of those enlisted. Among those who expressed an aided propensity, 28 percent took the ASVAB, and 13 percent of those enlisted. Thus between 28 and 50 percent acted on their propensity and 13 to 33 percent of those who took the ASVAB enlisted. Alternatively, only 14 percent of those indicating a negative propensity took the ASVAB, and only 5 percent of them enlisted. Orvis and Asch also estimate that a 10 percent decline in propensity translates into a 4 percent decline in enlistments. Finally, there are significant differences in propensity based on race, ethnicity, and gender.

DOD propensity data provided to me through the US Army Recruiting Command at Fort Knox, Kentucky, lays out a clear picture of propensity trends broken down by gender. In 1984, the male propensity was 24 percent, reaching a high of 27 percent in 1989 and a low of 12 percent in 2007. In 2011 it was 18 percent, a 25 percent drop from 1984 to 2011. Female propensity in 1984 was 10 percent, which represented an all-time high; the low was 4 percent in 2007. In 2011 it was 5 percent, a 50 percent drop from 1984. Aggregated, the propensity in 1984 was 17 percent, with a high of 18 percent in 1986–1988 and a low of 9 percent in 2008. Aggregate propensity in 2011 was 12 percent, a 29 percent drop since 1984. Here are the propensities presented in another format:

	1984	2011	Decline	High	Low
Male	24%	18%	25%	27% (1989)	12% (2007)
Female:	10%	5%	50%	10% (1984)	4% (2007)
Aggregate	17%	12%	29%	18% (1986–88)	9% (2008)

Neither the verbal nor tabular presentation is encouraging. It is also noteworthy that all of the high-propensity years were in the 1980s and the lows in the 2000s. Similar social and ethnic trends from 1984 to 2011 appear in the same DOD data. The propensity of white respondents fell 25 percent, from 12 percent to 9 percent; that of African Americans fell 48 percent, from 33 percent to 17 percent; and that of Hispanics fell 40 percent, from 27 percent to 16 percent.

Propensity is influenced by a number of factors. Perceived opportunities for higher education and civilian employment; the influence of parents, coaches, and friends; and the individual's knowledge of the military as a whole influence propensity. One of the most powerful influences is word of mouth from veterans and those currently serving. Recent experiences of stop-loss, PTSD, TBI, long and repeated deployments with little dwell time, suicides, unprecedented prescription of psychotropic drugs, and problems with the Veterans Administration do not help create a positive narrative from veterans or those still serving. In fact, a study ordered by the Center for Army Leadership at Fort Leavenworth, Kansas, conducted by ICF International in November and December 2011 informs this view. There were seventeen thousand responses. One out of every four soldiers serving in Afghanistan rated morale as low or very low. Most alarming, though, was the fact that only 25 percent of the respondents agreed with the statement, "The Army is headed in the right direction to prepare for the challenges of the next ten years." This was an all-time low, down from 38 percent in 2006 and 33 percent in 2010—an alarming trend.

If 30 percent of the eligible population is able to serve and 12 percent is willing, that means only 3.6 percent of the recruiting age market is likely to enter the military, and both elements of the equation have declined recently. Furthermore, this 3.6 percent figure includes only those who meet the *minimum* quality requirements. There is no reason to believe that those in the first socioeconomic quintile or at the high end of academic achievement will be any more likely to enlist than they have been in the past. The only substantive source of relief to recruiting pressures in the medium term will come from the planned downsizing of the force—a relief that will last only until the next war.

One final thought on recruiting into the military: it is extremely challenging for those assigned to recruiting duties. These are some of the hardest-working members of our military, and no one joined the military to be a recruiter. The job is made difficult by one other broad change in our society. Before 1973, one had to opt out of the military. All young men faced the reality that they might be required to serve in the military. Today, two generations of Americans have come to view military service as an opt-in arrangement. Participation is greater when people are forced to opt out of a program (for example, more employees participate in employer-offered 401k plans when they have to opt out than when they have to opt in). In their 2006 book *AWOL: The Unexcused Absence of America's Upper Class from Military Service*, authors Kathy Roth-Douquet (the wife of a career military officer) and Frank Schaeffer (the father of a Marine) address this issue:

> In the spring of 2005 the Army tried to do everything it could to avoid recasting the argument as to why people should volunteer. They raised recruiting bonuses to $40,000, offered to pay mortgages for the period of enlistment, dangled promises of a fast track to citizenship, raised the enlistment age to forty-two—just about anything short of winning a date with the general's daughter. The adjustments seemed to be working to the extent that by the end of 2005 fiscal year Army recruitment numbers were better than at the start of the year, even while the war in Iraq continued to lose public support. These efforts had all the appearances of hastily conceived and somewhat panicky Band-Aid "solutions."
>
> The old urgent, in-your-face World War II poster, "UNCLE SAM NEEDS YOU!" has been changed by today's military to read "Uncle Sam wants to make you a job offer you might consider. Got a better offer? Okay, sorry to have bothered you." Doesn't have much of a ring to it, does it?
>
> It seems to us that it is as demeaning and shortsighted to pitch the military as a sort of bonus program as it would be if the IRS began to offer mileage points to people who volunteered to pay their taxes. The idea of reducing patriotic duty to a matter of personal choice, job options, and perks on the one hand, while tacitly writing off Americans who can afford to ignore the bribes on the other, seems to us to spell trouble. But that is more or less what the military's recruiting policy is these days.

Since the recruiting methods are weighted in favor of the job-offer pitch, the military knows it can't compete with "job offers" made to prospective Ivy League graduates (averaging $50,000 starting salaries), so why bother? Besides which, it is too expensive to pay for those Ivy League tuitions; better to take kids from the state schools where the prices are cheaper. To us this seems to be a capitulation to cynicism.

In the long term, we as a country need to ask certain questions before we settle for the status quo. What do we lose under the status quo? We diminish the strength of our country's decision making. We lose because of the underdevelopment of character in the upper classes. And we diminish the long-term health of the military. And the military also loses future support.

There are fewer civilian leaders with knowledgeable, hands-on military experience. In other words, the military's future civilian bosses are going to be more ignorant than ever. If present statistical trends continue, we are fast approaching the day when no one in Congress and no president will have served or have any children serving.

If military leaders think this will be good for them and the men and women they lead, we beg to differ. We predict that the military will be overused and under led and that support will run out fast for any project that becomes a political liability. We predict that if the military leadership thinks that the men and women of the armed services were left twisting in the wind in the last years of the Vietnam War, as the saying goes, they ain't seen nothin' yet! There is a day of reckoning approaching when the military is going to be asked to do the impossible by very misinformed civilian leaders who will not be around to pick up the pieces.

Tom Brokaw endorsed their work, saying, *"AWOL is a powerful and timely account of those missing in action—the privileged class of America staying out of uniform and out of harm's way."*

The Next War

It may be soothing to tell a war-exhausted nation in 2013 that the United States will not engage in armed conflict on a large scale in the future. Believing this would require one to ignore history and look at a complex and threatening world through rose-colored glasses. The philosopher and writer George Santayana said, "Only the dead have seen the end of war." Our history since World War II is that we go to war on average every ten to twelve years (Korea in 1951, Vietnam in 1967, Desert Storm in 1991, Afghanistan in 2001, and Iraq in 2002). During much of this time, we also engaged in the Cold War with the Soviet Union, which consumed large portions of our national treasure and diplomatic energy. We also engaged in smaller exercises in military force in Lebanon, Grenada, Panama, the Balkans, Somalia, and Cuba. Magical thinking that ignores history should not drive national security debates.

Most Americans take pride and perhaps a measure of comfort that theirs is the most powerful military on the face of the earth, with global reach and technology that no other nation can match. This superiority comes at great expense, as the United States has a defense budget larger than that of the next fourteen countries in the world combined. Most of these fourteen are American allies. Only recently has defense spending come under rigorous scrutiny by the American public and Congress. It remains to be seen whether US defense spending will be reduced substantially.

A thoughtful skeptic of the idea that the United States possesses the most powerful military might look at that military's historical performance. If the purpose of the military is to fight and win America's wars, then it seems reasonable to evaluate how many wars it has won, lost, or fought to a tie. Our thoughtful skeptic might reasonably score Korea as a tie, Vietnam as a loss, Desert Storm as a win, Iraq as a loss, and Afghanistan as a loss or a tie. (Regarding Iraq, I should note that the 2012 Army Posture Statement signed by the secretary of the army and the army chief of staff stated that "we left Iraq responsibly." The word *win, won,* or *winning* never appeared, and the president never characterized the Iraq War as a US win.) So the skeptic's tally might be one win, two losses, and two ties or one win, three losses, and one tie, depending on whether Afghanistan is ultimately viewed as a tie or a loss. In completing the assessment, the skeptic might also note that we were successful against third-rate opposition in Panama (in 1989) and Grenada (in 1983) and were run out or chose to leave both Lebanon and Somalia in the post–World War II period. The skeptic might expect strong disagreement with his assessment, both informed and uninformed. The disagreement would probably include reasons for the outcomes that are not focused on the military: loss of public support, civilian meddling, and the lack of a clear mission. Nonetheless, the debate would be lively and should inform decisions to commit America's military in the future. It is unlikely that the technical competence, sacrifice, and commitment of the military's young enlisted soldiers and junior officers would be raised by either party in the debate. They routinely perform at their level of responsibility with distinction and courage.

It is not only our history of going to war frequently that informs the question of whether we are likely to do so in the future; it is also a mindset of militarism that has developed since the end of World War II. We have exercised our role as the world's self-proclaimed policeman through a policy of forward deployment of forces not seen since the Roman Empire, unprecedented capabilities of power projection, and frequent interventionism. We have come to summarize our position in most difficult diplomatic negotiations by saying, "The military option is still on the table," as if the secretary of state were the Godfather. In fact, in 1993 Secretary of State Madeleine Albright asked General Colin Powell, the chairman of the Joint Chiefs of Staff, "What's the point of having this superb military that you're always talking about if you can't use it?" Secretary Albright's question was preceded by a statement half a century earlier by an equally influential player, Henry R. Luce, who said in 1941 that his fellow citizens should "accept wholeheartedly our duty to exert upon the world the full impact of our influence for such purpose as we see fit and by such means as we see fit." [22]To a large extent, we appear to have taken Mr. Luce's exhortations to heart with mixed outcomes.

Militarism has become the centerpiece of US foreign policy and a focal point of international relations. After the debacle in Vietnam, the Weinberger doctrine emerged in the early 1980s. It provided that the United States would only go to war under five preconditions: the use of force would be restricted to matters of vital national interest; political and military objectives would be specific and achievable; the public and Congress would support the war; we would fight to win; and force would be a last resort. These principles were wise perhaps, but they were short-lived. In 2001, we adopted a military employment policy of preemptive and preventive war that appeared to violate every one of the principles of the Weinberger doctrine. These wars then led to mission creep, occupation, and expensive rebuilding of the countries we invaded, with the exit ramps for the United States difficult to find. While preventive wars and subsequent occupations drag on, we choose to initiate broader wars exercised with unmanned drones in Pakistan, Somalia, Yemen, and other sovereign nations, euphemistically categorizing the killing of their innocent citizens as collateral damage. Another emerging aspect of this ongoing exercise of militarism is cyber warfare. How would the US view and respond to a cyber attack like the one we executed against Iran with the Stuxnet virus? As we look at our past and the future, we might once again head the words of our founding fathers. James Madison wrote in 1795 in *Political Observations* that "no nation could preserve its freedom in the midst of continual warfare."

The relationship between militarism and the AVF is that the AVF has emerged as an enabler for militarism. The Gates Commission Report noted the objection that an all-volunteer force would encourage military operations and interventions, leading to an irresponsible national security policy and reducing civilian concerns about militarism. Their rebuttal

---

22 "The American Century", speech, 1941 (Mr. Luce is the founder of Time-Life Inc. and served as its publisher.

was that the entire force would be volunteers who would have no impact on the national command authority's decision to go to war or initiate military actions. They noted that domestic politics, financial costs, and the nature of threats to national security drive such decisions. Domestic politics has been overshadowed by militarism by both political parties. Concern for financial cost has been given lip service as the Pentagon budget has grown, and supplemental appropriations funded by rising debt to foreign creditors, China among them, have been common. The AVF has driven a very small portion of the American population to bear the total physical, social, and emotional cost of war in the name of those who have no skin in the game. **Alternative histories are difficult to write, but this one could be framed by asking the following question: If in 2004 or 2005, three years into the wars in Iraq and Afghanistan, the United States had activated the Selective Service System and begun conscripting enlistees into its military (including those from the first socioeconomic quintile), how long would either war have gone on? Similarly, if the federal government had imposed a war tax in 2004 on every US taxpayer, how long would the wars have gone on?**

Given the potential difficulties in manning the force in any future war, and recognizing the probability of the United States engaging in that war based on our history and embrace of militarism, the question is, War with whom? If we dismiss history and current ideology and believe that we will never again employ military force, the question is moot. Or if we discount recent history and believe that shock and awe will deliver short, decisive wars where we will be greeted as liberators, suffer minimum casualties, and the defeated enemy's resources will pay for the war (remember the assurances before the Iraq War), then the issue of how we man the force is less critical. These two irrational positions will collide with a different reality.

It is difficult if not impossible to predict against what country or countries the United States might fight in its next war or over what issue it may be fought. The short lists of most national security experts include Iran and North Korea in the medium term and China in the long term. I have included in Appendix 1 the population, land mass, and military strength of each of these three potential adversaries relative to the United States. Iran has a population greater than Iraq and Afghanistan combined and greater military strength than Iraq in 2003 as well as influence over the Straits of Hormuz, through which much of the world's oil passes. North Korea's military manpower is about equal to that of the United States. They have nuclear weapons, and a war with North Korea could draw in China. Neither of these totalitarian governments would be likely to sue for peace or surrender.

China presents a decidedly greater level of risk. Their population is four times greater than that of the United States, and their active military force is 50 percent larger. Their array of weapons systems, ships, and platforms (except for aircraft carriers) is comparable to that of the United States, and they have nuclear weapons and delivery systems for these weapons. China is unlikely to loan us the money to finance a war with them as they have our wars with Iraq and Afghanistan. Finally, China has recently embarked on a program to increase both the size and technological capability of its military.

In addition to the probability of engaging nation states like those mentioned above in traditional military conflicts, we face the prospect of the long war or the Global War on Terrorism. Although the quantity of recruits will not be as critical in this type of war, quality is extremely important. The current use of drones in countries like Afghanistan, Pakistan, Yemen, and Somalia requires service members at the upper ends of the intelligence distribution. And the emerging military aspects of cyberspace and the disruption of computer and communication networks may require even higher levels of intelligence and technical competence among our service members. In this area the military is engaged in a war for talent that it may be losing to the private sector or conceding to contractors driven by profit rather than patriotism.

In summary, the arguments above suggest three things. First, recruiting and retaining high-quality people into our all-volunteer military will not become any easier and may become more difficult in the future. Trends indicate there will be fewer willing to enlist, and obesity and high-school dropout rates predict there will be fewer who are able. Second, our history as a nation, our militarism, and our flirtation with preventive or preemptive war indicate that in a complex, threatening world, we will engage in significant combat operations in the future. Third, if we do engage in these significant combat operations, our likely foes will be capable and tenacious.

CHAPTER 7 - ALTERNATIVES

The All Volunteer Force is not fair, efficient, and sustainable. What are the options?

Winston Churchill, a statesman who knew a bit about war, said, "The statesman who yields to war fever is no longer the master of policy but the slave of unforeseeable and uncontrollable events." The question this book raises is not whether or how often to go to war but how to man the force. Is the AVF working—in other words, is it fair, efficient, and sustainable—and will it work in the future? This is a policy question to which the answers and alternatives are both foreseeable and controllable. In this chapter I will describe four widely discussed methods of manning the force and add a fifth from my own analysis of the question. I will include a description of each and an analysis of each based on the framework of fairness, efficiency, and sustainability.

Alternatives

Having discussed the history of how the United States has manned its military force, how we came to the method, and how that method has served America over the past forty years, it is appropriate to review the

AVF along with other alternatives. Unfortunately, recruiting is likely to become more difficult, and we are likely to confront a worthy opponent if and when we go to war. Thus the question of the AVF's effectiveness is relevant if not critical to national defense policy and the social fabric of our nation.

There are four commonly suggested approaches to dealing with the issue of manning our military forces. First is national service (either voluntary or mandatory), which proposes that all citizens, usually at age eighteen to twenty, give up to two years of service to the government either in the military or some other form of community service in the United States or overseas. This concept only indirectly addresses the issue of manning the military force, similar to the idea of the draft-induced volunteer of the Vietnam era. The concept does not generally require military service. Second is the concept of universal military training, according to which all citizens, upon completion of high school but no later than age twenty, would undergo basic military training of three to six months and then have no further obligation for military service except, perhaps, some reserve duty. Third is a lottery draft similar to that used in the United States from 1970 to 1973 that would feature limited deferments and could include women. Fourth is the all-volunteer model that we have explored in some detail. I will take the liberty of introducing a fifth alternative that draws on the strengths and weaknesses of the other four in the context of fairness, efficiency, and sustainability.

National Service

People often say that they are not in favor of the military draft but would favor national service. It is a concept that dates back to at least the early 1900s, when philosopher and psychologist William James wrote of a "moral equivalent of war" that would require young men to work for the community. He argued that "the martial values, although originally gained by the race through war, are absolute and permanent human goods" and that nonmilitary national service offered a means of capturing those values without going to war. Later in the century, anthropologist Margaret Mead weighed in on the Vietnam-era debate over the draft by stating that "Universal national service, in addition to solving the problem of fairness for those who are asked to serve in the military, in contrast to those who are not, is above all a new institution for creating responsible citizens alert to the problems and responsibilities of nationhood in a rapidly changing world." She went on to say that "Universal national service would provide an opportunity for young adults to establish an identity and a sense of self respect and responsibility as individuals before making career choices or establishing homes. At present a very large number go from dependency on their parents into careers that have been chosen for them, or use early marriage as a device to reach pseudo-adult status."

The concept of service to one's nation is difficult to fault and easy to embrace for philosophers and anthropologists. In fact, it is generally approved of in public opinion polls. Unfortunately, this utopian concept begins to lose its utility when confronted with the realities of definition, cost, administration, and second- and third-order effects on other segments of society. Another issue with the concept is whether national service should be voluntary or mandatory and whether it should be universal. One of the attractions of an ill-defined concept is that everyone can define it as they see fit and find comfort in doing so.

What is the likelihood that we as a nation could reach consensus on what should constitute national service—or that Congress could do so? How would we deal with the accusation of social engineering and bias as some agendas are supported and others are not? Would the national service program replace or augment existing faith-based institutions, and what if some of these existing organizations did not want to participate? Many needs may be identified. Who would decide which are to be addressed?

Depending upon the scope of the program and whether all eighteen- to twenty-year-olds would be required to serve, the cost could be enormous. Some estimates of a proposed program by the Clinton White House in the 1990s to enroll up to 150,000 people in a national service program placed the cost in excess of $2 billion per year. Another cost consideration would be the administration of a broadly expanded or universal program. Although some infrastructure already exists with the Peace Corps, Teach for America, AmeriCorps, and so on, it is likely that the expanded scope of services would require more administrative resources. In the view of some, these administrative resources would be labeled bureaucracy at a time when many politicians and pundits are criticizing big government.

The secondary effects of national service are easy to visualize and hard to quantify and balance. For example, who would decide who went to the military and who to a civilian agency if we were to institute mandatory universal national service, and by what criteria? Should postservice benefits be equal for military and civilian service? Could participants in national service programs replace government workers who are unionized? How would participants be evaluated and disciplined? What would be the effect on the fast food and other industries if hundreds of thousands of young people were removed from the civilian work force to national service programs? Finally, what would be the impact on existing faith-based or community-based volunteer programs? Would collaboration or competition prevail?

One reality with which the utopian vision of mandatory national service would collide is the US Constitution. The Thirteenth Amendment forbids not only slavery but also involuntary servitude. The involuntary servitude provision was included in the legislation to ensure that state governments would not reenslave African Americans by imposing temporary forced labor systems. Many constitutional scholars believe that nonmilitary mandatory national service is, in fact, involuntary servitude. It is reasonable to assume that the constitutionality of mandatory national service would be tested before a national program could be legislated, funded, and initiated.

Notwithstanding the practical concerns raised above, loosely defined utopian visions of national service arise in the minds not only of philosophers and anthropologists but also of legislators, presidents, and other government officials in Washington. The visions are often fueled by memories of Franklin Delano Roosevelt's Civilian Conservation Corps and John F. Kennedy's Peace Corps, neither of which were mandatory or universal or impacted how or how effectively we manned our military. In 1988 the Democratic Leadership Council, of which Governor Bill Clinton was a member, proposed a Citizens Corps of eight hundred thousand young people to perform tasks like filling out police paperwork or cleaning national parks. Benefits for the participants would be set by a corporation for national service and include education vouchers. President Clinton did not seek to implement candidate Clinton's vision; the cost was projected in the billions of dollars. In 2003, 2006, 2007, and 2010 Congressman Charles Rangel introduced legislation for a national service obligation, military or civilian, for every citizen between the ages of eighteen and forty-two. Military service would be a mandatory option only if the president declared a national emergency. The 2010 bill had no cosponsors, and none of these initiatives passed the House. This was one national service initiative that did, at least indirectly, address the military manning issue. Finally, the 2008 Generations Invigorating Volunteering and Education Act, known as the GIVE Act, promoted by President Obama, was a proposal to create 175,000 new service opportunities under AmeriCorps. It included new initiatives like a Clean Energy Corps, an Education Corps, a Healthy Futures Corps, and a Veterans Service Corps. The projected cost was $6 billion over five years. It made no mention of manning the military forces. The proposed act did not become law.

In summarizing the first concept for manning the force, national service, I will offer an analysis of its fairness, efficiency, and sustainability. I trust that the engaged reader will develop his or her own analysis.

- **Fairness.** The utopian model of national service that is both mandatory and universal is arguably fair. If it is not mandatory and universal, the fairness argument begins to weaken. It weakens further as those who serve are assigned to either military or civilian functions, given the inherent risks of military service. Even within civilian assignments, some are more attractive than others; working as a clerk in a police station is more attractive than picking up roadside trash to most people. Who decides who will be assigned where? However, despite these caveats, national service is arguably fair.

- **Efficiency.** Most national service models are expensive, as they include a minimum living stipend, health insurance, and some aid for education after serving or education loan forgiveness. In addition, a mandatory universal program would require some administrative structure that would add cost to the program. These costs would be weighed against the economic benefit of the work performed and the intangible benefits to the participants (maturity, patriotism, and so on) and the nation. In a country with $16 trillion in debt, this would be a challenging sell. Finally, it does not clearly answer the question of manning the force, as some may argue that they are willing to perform civilian service but not military service. The administrative requirements of national service render it inefficient.

- **Sustainability.** It is difficult to speculate whether something that has never existed is sustainable. The fact that in our 240-year-old republic it has never been implemented argues against its sustainability. The Thirteenth Amendment's provision against involuntary servitude would challenge its sustainability. Power shifts in Washington, changes in public opinion and values, and budget pressures also argue against the sustainability of universal national service programs. National service is not sustainable.

Universal Military Training

Universal military training (UMT) is a concept of manning the force in which every male (and in some models every female), upon reaching a certain age, is required to undergo military training for some short period and then serve in the nation's active or reserve force for some period of time. In most models of UMT, exemption and deferments

138

are rare. UMT is utopian in some ways and pragmatic in others. It is utopian in that it equally shares the burden and risk of military service among all citizens, increases the sense of citizenship, accelerates the maturing process of a nation's youth, teaches discipline, and enhances social cohesion. It is pragmatic in that it directly generates military manpower sufficient to provide national security, can reduce military personnel costs, can reduce the gap between the military and civilian society, and makes the decision to go to war more of a national decision, as it eliminates the ability of the socioeconomic elite to avoid risk.

In the United States, UMT is most closely associated with President Harry Truman. On October 23, 1945, Truman went before a joint session of Congress and asked the legislators to establish a system of UMT for the United States. His proposal was that every young man between the ages of eighteen and twenty undergo one year of military training and then serve six years in the reserve system. His own secretary of war urged him to delay the proposal, but Truman felt that action was necessary "while the nation can still see the ravages and ruin of war" and was concerned with a menacing Soviet Union. But Congress saw things differently, as they were concerned with demobilization, the creation of the United Nations, and the implications of atomic weapons. Furthermore, the American public was focused on a return to normalcy after the war. Congress did not act on the proposal.

Truman continued to advocate for UMT in the ensuing years, but on August 29, 1950, he wrote a letter to the chairmen of the House and Senate Armed Services Committees which addresses the fairness, efficiency, and sustainability of the concept. The letter reads in part,

> I am very much in favor of universal training legislation. The record will show that for the past five years I have repeatedly recommended that the Congress enact legislation of this character. I am just as strongly in favor of it today as I have ever been.
>
> However, the realities of the situation are that if such legislation were enacted tomorrow it could not possibly be

put into effect at once. A universal training program would require many training camps and other installations and scores of thousands of experienced military personnel for training purposes. In view of the demands made on our military forces by the Korea aggression, it is clear that we could not possibly make available the installation and trained military manpower to put a universal training program into operation at this time or in the immediate foreseeable future. Accordingly, it does not seem to me immediately necessary for Congress to enact universal training legislation.

With this 1950 letter, UMT was largely laid to rest as a method of manning the US military. The concept was raised briefly in 1966 by prominent military sociologists Morris Janowitz of the University of Chicago and Charles Moskos of Northwestern University as part of the draft debate. A final call for UMT was sounded by highly decorated Vietnam veteran, military journalist, and author Colonel David Hackworth in September of 1999, when he suggested that it would be a means to shape up America's youth and restore patriotic values.

Despite the failure of UMT to gain traction as a means of manning the US military, it is the preferred method in some other democracies. These include Israel, South Korea, and Singapore. All three countries are much smaller than the United States, all face military threats more imminent than the United States, and none have the same range of global commitments as the United States.

In Israel, all men and women are required to enter the military at age eighteen (men for three years and women for two years). Arab citizens and the ultraorthodox religious are exempted. Upon completion of initial active service, members may remain in the active service or go to the reserve, where they are subject to up to one month of duty per year until age forty-three. Competition for assignment to elite units is intense, with the needs of the Israeli Defense Force determining individual assignments. In South Korea, only males between the ages of eighteen and thirty-five are subject to UMT for periods of twenty-one to thirty-six months. Wages are very low, and Olympic athletes are exempt. In Singapore, all able-bodied males between the ages of eighteen and twenty-one are subject to twenty-four months of active military service and then reserve training cycles of up to forty days per year for the next ten years. Clearly, there is a lot more skin in the game in these three countries than in the United States.

The table below compares the United States with these three nations in terms of population, size of active forces, size of reserve forces, and the percentage of the total population assigned to each.

	Total Pop.	Active Force	% of Total Pop.	Reserve Force	% of Total Pop.
United States	315 million	1.4 Mil.	.04%	1.4 million	.04%
Israel	7.9 million	176,000	2.2%	445,000	5.6%
S. Korea	50.5 million	639,000	1.2%	2.9 million	5.8%
Singapore	5.0 million	71,000	1.3%	350,000	6.6%

At this point basic arithmetic appears to overwhelm both utopian visions and pragmatic arguments. If a percentage of the US population comparable to that of any of these nations were required to serve, our active forces would rise from 1.4 million to 4.2 million. Put another way, approximately 2.1 million people reach military age each year in the United States. If 30 percent were fit to serve, that would mean inducting and training 630,000 people per year. In two years, we would almost double the size of our active force, and the impact is exponential thereafter depending on the number of years of required service in the active and reserve components. This reflects the constraint to which President Truman referred in his 1950 letter to Congress when he wrote, "we could not possibly make available the installation and scores of thousands of experienced military personnel for training purposes." The arithmetic dictates that supply would exceed demand and requirements. More arithmetic dictates that a deeply indebted nation could not afford it.

My summary of UMT as a means of manning the force in terms of its fairness, efficiency, and sustainability follows. The reader is, of course, invited to make his or her own assessment.

- **Fairness.** In its pure form, it is fair—perhaps more so than any other model—and has utopian and pragmatic appeal. The only significant open question regarding fairness is whether both men and women would be subject to universal military training. UMT is fair.
- **Efficiency.**_Utopian idealism collides with arithmetic, and arithmetic wins. UMT generates a force larger than required and requires a training base, in terms of installations and personnel, two to three times larger than the one currently in place. Finally, the budget and economic cost to create and sustain something that is not required is totally unjustifiable. UMT is not efficient in the United States.
- **Sustainability.** The efficiency summary above and exponential growth in the size of the force that would occur over just a few years leads to the conclusion that UMT is absolutely unsustainable.

Conscription

In 1973, America changed two long-standing social policies. One change allowed women to terminate unwanted pregnancies, and it has been debated continually by pundits, political candidates, legislators, and activists since Roe v. Wade was decided by the Supreme Court on January 22, 1973. The other change was the end of the draft and the official implementation of the AVF on July 1, 1973. The end of the draft represented a legislated termination of the moral obligation of citizens to defend the nation. Before 1973, every American male was obligated to serve if called. The paradigm of military service shifted from one where Americans were required to opt out of military service to one where they were invited to opt in. Since 1973, there has been little debate about the fairness, efficiency, or sustainability

of the decision to end the draft or whether the draft was sacrificed to atone for the political and strategic sins of the Vietnam War.

Since 1973, debate and dialogue regarding the draft have been intermittent and brief. Charles Moskos, a professor of sociology at Northwestern University and a former draftee, wrote an article in the *Washington Monthly* in November 2001 entitled "Now Do You Believe We Need a Draft?" In the article, he states:

> Part of what makes Americans dubious of conscription is our memory of how the class based draft of the Vietnam War-era helped drive America apart. We tend to forget that the more equitable draft that existed during World War II and for 20 years afterwards helped bring the country together. During the peaceful years of the 1950's ... a time not unlike our own, when the threat of mass destruction hung in the air ... most Ivy League men had to spend two years in uniform, before or after college, working and bunking with others of very different background and races (the military, remember, was about the only racially integrated institution at the time). This shared experience helped instill in those who served, as in the national culture generally, a sense of unity and moral seriousness that we would not see again ... until after September 11, 2001.

The surge of post-9/11 patriotism that caused Americans to opt in to the AVF was short-lived, and the military soon saw enlistment shortfalls. In the same *Washington Monthly* article, Moskos writes,

> Reinstituting the draft is the obvious way to meet the suddenly increased manpower needs for military and homeland security. This fact would have seemed obvious to previous generations of Americans. That today we aren't even talking about a draft is a measure of the deep psychological resistance Americans have developed to anything that smacks of the state compelling anyone to do anything. Ideology plays a role here. In general the

left doesn't like the military, and the right doesn't like anything that interferes with the marketplace. When it comes to national needs, the left believes in something for nothing, the right in every man for himself.

The psychological resistance also gains comfort from arguments made by opponents of the draft and by the military hierarchy, which also resists a return to conscription (the military resists the draft largely because it resists all change; it opposed ending the draft in 1973).

One argument is that today's military requires professional soldiers, especially for overseas missions. Let's leave aside the fact that in World War II, Korea, and Vietnam most combat soldiers had only six months of training before being sent to war.

Dr. Moskos was a deep thinker and strong advocate for his views, but he had no real power to shape policy, and those who did shape policy often substituted sound bites for informed dialogue. On March 7, 2003, Secretary of Defense Donald Rumsfeld, asked about a return to conscription, dismissed the service member of the pre AVF military as "adding no value, no advantage, really, to the United States armed services." He added that the "churning that took place took an enormous amount of effort in terms of training, and then they were gone." It's reasonable to think that many of those who "added no value" as conscripts in World War II, Korea, and Vietnam saw it differently. One of those who spoke out was Senator Chuck Hagel, who on April 20, 2004, called for a return to conscription (Senator Hagel now serves as the secretary of defense). In the Senate Foreign Relations Committee, of which he was a member, Hagel asked, "why shouldn't we ask all our citizens to bear some responsibility and pay some price?" He went on to say that the draft would force "our citizens to understand the intensity and depth of challenges we face." Hagel also noted that "those who are serving today and dying today are the middle class and lower class" and that reinstituting the draft would cause the burden of military service to be spread among all economic classes of people. Finally, even the last vestiges of the draft are under attack as two congressmen, Peter Defazeo of Oregon (a Democrat) and Mike Coffman of Colorado (a Republican), proposed in February of 2012 that the Selective Service be abolished in order to save its $24 million annual budget.[23]

Earlier in this book we reviewed the history and pros and cons of conscription as a means to man the nation's military forces; there is no need to repeat that discussion here. For the past forty years, the American people and their leaders have rejected conscription. Most people, as a result of fear, apathy, ignorance, or guilt, give it no serious thought. Why would they? They have no skin in the game. My analysis of conscription follows:

- **Fairness.** The fairness of conscription can be debated at several levels. At the highest level of social theory, libertarians would argue that any time governments impose themselves on the lives and liberties of their citizens it is unfair, immoral, and undemocratic. Those who view conscription through the examples of the Civil War commutation and substitution laws and the abuse of deferments in the Vietnam era would argue that conscription under these conditions was unfair. They would justifiably raise the issue of the rich man's war and the poor man's fight. Others may argue that it is unfair to conscript men only, as women make up a large portion of the AVF and advocate for ending the combat exclusion rules for women. On the other hand, one can argue that a national lottery to identify and enlist conscripts with no deferments for both men and women (with women assigned to combat arms only if they volunteer for combat arms and meet gender-neutral standards) would be a democratic and fair method of manning the force. I should note that even if conscription was reinstated, volunteers would still make up the majority of the force. Of one thing we may be certain: if all these

---

23 "Lawmakers Seek End to Draft Registration", Military.com daily news, February 25, 2013

diverse views about the fairness of conscription are confronted by the reality of an existential military threat to the United States requiring the full mobilization of the nation's military-age population, we will embrace conscription; survival will define fairness. The draft as executed from 1970 to 1973 was not fair, as it offered too many exemptions and deferments and did not include women. Conscription by lottery with no exemptions or deferments is fair.

- **Efficiency.** Measured in budgetary terms, conscription was efficient. It provided manpower at reasonable rates of pay and benefits to enlistees who had no military skills. Conscripted enlistees were not paid cash enlistment bonuses. And in most cases, conscripted enlistees were young and did not have dependents who claimed government health care and other dependent benefits. Measured in strategic terms, conscription was efficient in that it gave Pentagon manpower planners a predictable flow of enlistees to make up any gap between manpower requirements and volunteers. Manpower planners were not at the mercy of the civilian unemployment rate, casualty statistics, or the allocation of enlistment bonus funds from Congress.

Finally, there is the issue of budget costs versus economic costs raised by economists on the Gates Commission. Their argument was that conscription caused the national economy to incur costs that were not identified in the defense budget. These economic costs exist no matter what method is used to man the force; the only difference is the way these costs are distributed. The economic cost argument is also addressed by Dr. Joseph Stinglitz and Linda Bilmes in their book *The Three Trillion Dollar War*, in which the authors identify the true costs of the wars in Iraq and Afghanistan and some of the costs that were a direct or indirect effect of the way we manned the military. (I strongly recommend the book to those interested in the economics of national defense.) In closing, I would argue that conscription is efficient in both strategic and financial terms.

- **Sustainability.** The sustainability of conscription as a method to man our military force is open to debate. From 1862 until 1973, conscription was sustainable and provided sufficient manpower to fight the nation's wars and send a message of readiness to the Soviets during the Cold War. Notwithstanding Secretary Rumsfeld's disparaging assessment of conscripts, the only war conscripted armies lost was the Vietnam War. The other side of the sustainability argument is that after Vietnam, conscription was not sustainable, and for forty years we have used other means to man our forces. This dichotomy speaks to the central question of this book. Conscription as we have executed it in the past is not sustainable except in cases of total mobilization. If political will or the threat is sufficient, conscription is sustainable.

The All-Volunteer Force

A compelling illusion exists that the AVF is working. We have generally been able to man the force to meet strength requirements and provide sufficient forces to combatant commanders over sustained periods of war. The only periods in which these conditions did not prevail were the mid to late 1970s when the DOD was making the transition from conscription to the AVF while dealing with the lingering effects from the Vietnam War and the period from 2005 to 2007 at the height of the wars in Iraq and Afghanistan. In both cases policy adjustments were made to deal with the shortfalls. In the former case, the response was improved compensation and benefits—a generally positive, sustainable response. In the latter case the response was bonuses, repeat deployments, lowered standards, use of prescription psychotropic drugs, stop-loss, and other policies of questionable ethical legitimacy and sustainability. Ethics and sustainability aside, the AVF worked at least at the strategic or policy level; whether it worked for the thousands of service members and their families who were affected by these policies is another question.

It also works for the American public, as they have been granted a mass exemption by Congress from any military service, thus becoming limited liability patriots who can voice support and respect for the troops while going about their day-to-day business. They are not required to opt out but are invited to opt in, and few who have other alternatives choose to do so. It works, too, for a generally risk-averse senior military (the senior military resisted racial integration, gender integration, and the AVF) that is dependent on Congress for individual promotions and budgets and therefore is reluctant to question the AVF, as the question is politically difficult for Congress—a rational quid pro quo. The AVF also works for the military because it is theoretically easier to lead and discipline a service member who wants to be in the military for patriotic or financial reasons than one who is conscripted. Nonetheless, from 1862 until 1973, US military leaders at all levels were able to lead, motivate, and discipline conscripts. The only war conscripted American militaries ever lost was Vietnam. The AVF also works for Congress, as it reflects the perceived values and personal interests of its constituents, leading legislators to provide funding and policies to support the AVF. The AVF also works for Congress and most senior government officials because most of them opted out of military service. Thus, calling into question the ethics or efficacy of the AVF could be self-incriminating or hypocritical at worst and uncomfortable at best. Finally, the argument is reinforced by the tyranny of the status quo. Why question the status quo or explore alternatives if something is believed to be working?

The counterarguments to the AVF as a preferred means of manning our military are compelling. First, the AVF facilitates the civilian-military gap outlined in the first chapter of this book. The professional military that draws its members disproportionately from the middle and lower socioeconomic classes becomes estranged from the society it serves. Senior civilian leaders in government, business, and the press have difficulty understanding and relating to military issues and are sometimes intimidated by uniformed senior leaders. And some in the military consciously or unconsciously look down on civilians as undisciplined, self-interested, and unpatriotic. Second, personnel costs of the AVF make it unsustainable. Fiscal reality cannot be ignored by a debt- and deficit-burdened America. Third, the AVF makes the decision to go to war and remain at war easier for senior leaders, both civilian and military. It is easier for a nation to maintain public support for a war when the majority of the citizens have no skin in the game. I maintain that if we had heeded Secretary (then Senator) Chuck Hagel's call for conscription in 2004, we would have been out of both Iraq and Afghanistan in 2005 or 2006. Finally, the consequences of the policies implemented to support the AVF during this last decade of war (PTSD, a suicide crisis, widespread prescription drug addiction, and others) should cause a responsible nation to ask whether the means to support the AVF justified the ends. Would the nation have benefited from an open, informed dialogue regarding these means and ends and alternatives? That's a discussion for the next section of this chapter. For now, I'll proceed to a summary of the AVF's fairness, efficiency, and sustainability.

- **Fairness.** Conceptually, the all-volunteer model is fair; in practice, it is not. Every American who chooses to volunteer and meets the entry standards can enlist. No American is forced to do something he or she does not want to do. Similarly, every citizen in Pittsburgh can choose to sleep under one of its many bridges on a cold January night. In each case, some people have a broader range of options than others. If it is a voluntary force, why do we pay enlistment bonuses? **No volunteer model can be considered fair if its primary means of generating more volunteers is to provide financial incentives (enlistment and reenlistment bonuses) that are disproportionately attractive to members of the lower socioeconomic classes and irrelevant to socioeconomic elites.** The difference is that in the case of the military, every citizen theoretically benefits from the security provided by those who choose to serve. The AVF creates a legal and perhaps moral justification for this free-rider status. The fairness assessment also must acknowledge the disproportionate risk and sacrifice borne by service members, veterans, and military families. The AVF is not fair. No system that institutionalizes the practice of poor men fighting rich men's wars can be considered fair in a democracy.

- **Efficiency.** Strategically, the AVF has proven to be inefficient, because the force cannot be expanded to meet operational requirements as demonstrated in Iraq and Afghanistan. This inability forced the Pentagon to violate policies regarding dwell times, use of prescription psychotropic drugs, and enlistment standards. These violations have secondary effects on morale, discipline, and cost. Costs of the AVF are also higher than those of a conscripted force due to enlistment bonuses. Costs are also higher in the AVF because the force is older and therefore includes more members with spouses and children, all of whom are beneficiaries of high-quality military health care and other benefits. In advocating for a return to conscription, Charles Moskos wrote in the previously cited 2001 article,

> Draftees would not have to be offered the relatively high wages and benefits that it takes to lure voluntary recruits (an increasing number of whom are married with families). This would leave more funds available to raise pay for the kinds of personnel that the military is having a terrible hard time holding on to, such as computer specialists, mid-level officers, and master sergeants. To put it boldly, we now have overpaid recruits and underpaid sergeants. In the draft era, the pay ratio between a master sergeant and a private was seven to one; today it is less than three to one. Restoring something like the old balance is the best way to upgrade retention in hard-to-fill skills and leadership positions.

The inherent inability to expand the force to meet end strength requirements without violating established policies and standards and the significantly higher overall personnel costs of a volunteer force render the AVF strategically and economically inefficient.

- **Sustainability**. The sustainability of the AVF has been questioned from time to time. But it was never so unambiguously questioned as when President Richard Nixon, arguably the father of the AVF, wrote in his 1980 book *The Real War,*

> I considered the end of the draft in 1973 to be one of the major achievements of my administration. Now, seven years later, I have reluctantly concluded that we should reintroduce the draft. The need for the United States to project a strong military posture is now urgent, and the volunteer army has failed to provide enough personnel of the caliber we need for our highly sophisticated armaments. Its burden should be shared equally by all strata of society, with random selection and as few deferments as possible.[24]

President Nixon could not foresee the collapse of the Soviet Union in 1989 that created the peace dividend and allowed the United States to dramatically reduce its military personnel requirements. Nor could he anticipate the personnel policies that were employed to support the wars in Iraq and Afghanistan. Nonetheless, his analysis is relevant today; it will be even more relevant, perhaps, tomorrow.

Personnel costs also inform the question of the sustainability of the AVF. Notwithstanding the Gates Commission's assessment and assurances forty years ago, the AVF has become unbearably expensive for a debt-burdened nation. In a July 2012 report, the Center for Strategic and Budgetary Assessment stated, "Over the past decade, the cost per person in the active duty force increased by 46 percent. If personnel costs continue to grow at that rate and the overall defense budget remains flat with inflation, military personnel costs will consume the entire

---

[24] "The Real War", Richard Nixon, Simon & Schuster, Inc., NewYork, 1980, p.201.

defense budget by 2039." Further, the Reserve Forces Policy Board in a January 2013 report to the secretary of defense stated that "The fully burdened and life-cycle cost trends supporting the current AVF are unsustainable. The Secretary of Defense, current and former DoD officials, and prominent think tanks alike have all underscored this problem." Finally, Secretary of Defense Leon Panetta stated that "the escalating growth in personnel costs must be confronted. This is an area of the budget that has grown by nearly 90 percent since 2001." From a cost standpoint, the AVF is unsustainable.

Based on the perception that the AVF has worked for forty years, one could argue that it will work in the future. But past is not necessarily prologue. The argument that the AVF has worked in the past must face the reality of a decreasing propensity to serve among America's youth; only three out of ten are qualified to serve. The pool of veterans who might influence the next generation to volunteer is shrinking. The lingering effects of stop-loss and other policies will make recruiting high-quality enlistees more difficult as will the ongoing failure of the military to deal effectively with sexual violence. The unprecedented backlog of claims and long processing times at the Veterans Administration also makes military service less attractive. Skyrocketing personnel costs are not sustainable. Finally, even if we are capable of fighting the next war with the AVF, we must ask ourselves as a nation whether doing so would be morally justified, knowing the impact that these last twelve years of war have had on individual service members and their families and the social fabric of our democracy. If not, are we willing to explore alternatives?

A final question regarding the sustainability of the AVF is this: What if we had a war and nobody on our side showed up? This question alone causes me to argue that the AVF is not sustainable.

A Fifth Alternative

Since none of the four widely advocated or executed models of manning the force fully satisfy the criteria of fairness, efficiency, and sustainability, a fifth alternative may be appropriate. Each of the first four offers strengths and weaknesses that should be leveraged and addressed. The alternative should draw on existing DOD practices and policies and studies by respected analysts on national security issues. Finally, the alternative should address not only the implications on service members but also fiscal and war-fighting realities. The alternative is based on four elements: changing the mix of active and reserve-component ground forces, leveraging the cost savings of this change, aggressively executing and resourcing the Pentagon's ARFORGEN model, and introducing conscription into the reserve components.

Currently, the United States faces no existential threats but does operate in a threat environment that is unpredictable, disorderly, and disruptive. Nonetheless we continue to employ a Cold War twentieth-century defense strategy that is based on forward presence, power projection, and intervention. In addition to 68,000 troops in Afghanistan, we have approximately 60,000 thousand in Europe, 50,000 in Japan, and almost 30,000 in South Korea, a very expensive forward presence. In a February 2013 paper titled "National Defense in a Time of Change," retired Admiral Gary Roughead (former chief of naval operations) and Kori Schake of the Hoover Institution address the force mix. They recommend that the navy and air force remain at current end strength levels that would maintain the US capability to project force while significantly reducing the size of US ground forces. They recommend that the active component of the US Army be reduced by 200,000 soldiers from the 490,000 reflected in the fiscal year 2013 budget and that the Marine Corps be reduced by 28,000 from the 200,000 reflected in the budget. The active component of the army would then have an end strength of 290,000, and the Marine Corps end strength would be 172,000. Even at these reduced levels, US active-duty ground forces would still represent almost half a million service members. The authors also recommend increasing the end strengths of the National Guard and Army Reserve by 100,000 positions (currently the National Guard strength is approximately 350,000 and the Army Reserve is 200,000). In this model, total US ground forces would be more than 1.1 million. The authors acknowledge that these reductions would violate the tradition of balanced reductions among services but point out that they are justified by strategic and fiscal realities (I outline the fiscal impacts of this force mix in the next section). Inherent in this force mix model is the additional cost savings of closing some US installations overseas.

The second element of this alternative involves cost. As noted previously, the Reserve Forces Policy Board study states that "The fully burdened life cycle cost trends supporting the current All Volunteer Force are unsustainable. The Secretary of Defense, current and former senior DoD officials, and prominent think tanks alike have all underscored the problem." Personnel costs under the AVF have grown nearly 90 percent since 2001, primarily due to health-care and retirement costs, while the size of the force has remained approximately the same. At this rate, if the overall defense budget remains flat with inflation, by 2039 military personnel costs will consume the entire defense budget. The Reserve Force Policy Board study identified the fully burdened life-cycle costs of an active-duty service member and a reserve-component service member. The study found that the annual fully burdened life-cycle cost of the active-component service member was $384,622 and the cost of the reserve-component service member was $123,622. This stunning difference of $261,000 is primarily driven by health care, retirement, and dependent support costs. I have included in Appendix 2 the detailed elements of the cost difference. Applying this cost difference to the force mix of active-component and reserve-component soldiers previously outlined in the Bookings Institution policy brief represents significant cost reductions:

Army active-component force reduction of 200,000 positions	x $384,622 = $76.9 billion
Marine Corps force reduction of 28,000 positions	x $384,622 = $10.7 billion
	Total $87.6 billion
Addition of 100,000 reserve-component positions x $123,622	$12.3 billion
Total personnel cost reduction (net saving)	$75.3 billion

Even if the Reserve Forces Policy Board analysis is off by a factor of two (which is unlikely, given the rigor and scope of its analysis), a savings between $37 and $75 billion per year is impossible for a deficit- and debt-challenged nation to ignore. If military personnel planners chose to make the force mix change from active component to reserve component a one-for-one swap and added two hundred thousand reserve component positions instead of one hundred thousand, the savings would be $63 billion.

A thoughtful reader who is not familiar with the army may wonder why the army would not embrace this alternative. The army is an authoritarian bureaucracy at its highest levels. It is headed by the army chief of staff. He and his entire senior staff have spent their entire adult lives in the active component of the army. He has been personally and professionally affirmed by the active component of the army. His identity is linked to this institution, and most of his friends and colleagues are part of this cloistered priesthood. Thus, he would be disinclined to have as his legacy proposing, advocating for, and presiding over an unprecedented reduction in the size of the active component of the army; he would be a military heretic. Additionally, one may ask why the senior leader of the reserve component would not propose and advocate for this alternative. He reports to the army chief of staff. His budget and the promotions of his entire staff are subject to the approval of the army chief of staff. Creative thinking and expression of dissenting opinions from subordinates in an authoritarian bureaucracy are neither welcome nor career enhancing. Even those wearing three or four stars on their uniforms are subject to the human frailties of ego, bias, and survival instinct. The system is perfectly designed to produce suboptimal thinking and protect the status quo.

The third element of this alternative is the strategic reliance on the reserve components, particularly for ground combat capabilities. Prior to 2001, this heavier reliance on reserve-component forces would have been met with skepticism. The reserve component has proven to be an effective military instrument in Iraq and Afghanistan. By Pentagon policy, they are no longer weekend warriors. They are an operational reserve. This alternative reflects that status. The ability of the reserve components to execute their military missions has been clearly demonstrated over the past twelve years of war. When the reserve component morphed from a strategic to an operational reserve in 2004 through 2006, the army changed the model of how the reserve component trained and prepared for mobilization and deployment. The strategic reserve training model focused on tiered readiness in which only a small portion of the total reserve-component force was deployable at one time. The new training, mobilization, and deployment model is called army force generation (ARFORGEN). The ARFORGEN process gives substance to the change from a strategic to an operational reserve by having units move through a five-year cycle of progressively more rigorous, broader, and more heavily resourced training for four years, reaching a deployable level of readiness and proficiency in the fifth year. All of this preparation occurs during monthly drills and annual training (usually two weeks). The Army National Guard noted in its August 1, 2011, white paper "Implementing the Army Force Generation Model in the Army National Guard" that post mobilization training of all units other than aviation would be no greater than thirty to forty-five days. Therefore, a reserve component unit as large as a brigade combat team in the fifth year of the ARFORGEN training cycle could move from its hometown to a combat zone anywhere in the world in thirty to forty-five days according to the National Guard white paper. For ARFORGEN to function predictably and on a sustained basis, a stable and steady stream of trained personnel is critical. The model provides substantial and sustainable surge capability.

The result of this force mix and the ARFORGEN model on the Pentagon's ability to generate and sustain ground combat forces is that at any time the US Army can deploy up to one-third of its active-duty strength of 290,000 and one-fifth of its reserve-component strength of 650,000, a total of 225,000 trained soldiers in no more than forty-five days. Additionally, the Marine Corps could deploy more than 57,000 troops immediately. Rarely in our nation's history has the military been required to respond more quickly or in greater numbers. This level of readiness is provided at a cost savings of billions of taxpayer dollars.

The fourth element of this alternative is a requirement for stability of personnel assigned to reserve-component units through the ARFORGEN training cycle and a predictable, sustainable flow of high-quality recruits into the armed forces. Therefore, I recommend that the United States initiate a lottery-based draft into the Army National Guard and the Army Reserve of all citizens, men and women, in the year of their eighteenth birthday. Those called and qualified would have three options. The first is to serve six years in the reserve component after basic training (which could be completed between high-school graduation and college entry). If while serving as a conscripted soldier in the reserve components during the six-year commitment, that soldier is mobilized and deployed for one year, their military commitment is complete, and they can leave the military. Second, the individual could choose to serve two years after basic and advanced individual training in the active army or Marine Corps, a commitment of approximately two-and-one-half years. Third, the individual could choose to go directly to college but must be enrolled in an ROTC program and meet the requirements for commissioning. This would significantly improve the quality of ROTC cadets across all services and thus improve the quality of the young officers who have the privilege and responsibility of leading our sons and daughters. If an individual who chooses this option leaves the ROTC program or fails to meet commissioning requirements, he or she would be required to choose one of the other two options at the end of that semester. Conscripted soldiers would not be eligible for any enlistment bonuses. With approximately two million Americans turning eighteen each year, a relatively small number would be conscripted (unless total war broke out), but they would be of high quality and include members of every socioeconomic quintile. Voluntary enlistment of nonconscripts would continue to be strongly encouraged, and they would likely make up a majority of both active-duty and reserve-component forces.

Meaningful adverse consequences for those conscripts who fail to fulfill their military obligation would be required to make this concept work. Those consequences would have to be effective for all socioeconomic classes. I recommend several: the permanent suspension of the privilege to vote and hold public office, the denial of admission to any public institution of higher learning, and the denial of any government benefits other than those to which the individual directly contributes, such as Social Security and Medicare. Additionally, the failure to report for induction if selected should result in a speedy felony conviction punishable by one weekend per month and two weeks each summer for six years in a local county jail, with the incarcerated draft dodger obligated to reimburse the county for meals served. Finally, I suspect that the military may object to conscripts in its ranks on the grounds that they will be more difficult to motivate, train, and discipline than volunteers, despite its claim to strong leadership capabilities. In response, I point out that generations of military leaders motivated, trained, and disciplined conscripts and won the Civil War, World War I, World War II, and the Cold War with conscripts. A Marine drill instructor at Parris Island once told me that "anyone can lead a thirsty horse to water. Good drill instructors can get those who aren't thirsty to drink, and a great drill instructor can get them to like it."

My assessment of this alternative's fairness, efficiency, and sustainability follows.

- **Fairness.** If, in order to be fair, all must serve or none must serve, then none of the alternatives are fair as a practical matter. The supply of potential service members, given the large population of the United States, far exceeds demand. **If, on the other hand, fairness is defined as every American, male and female, upon reaching the age of eighteen, having the potential to be called to military service without exemptions or deferments, then this alternative is fair. It causes the children and grandchildren of congressmen and CEO's to have as much skin in the game as those of forklift drivers and firemen.** To some extent, this addresses the old phrase "a rich man's war and a poor man's fight." Additionally, the voices of the first socioeconomic quintile may be heard as we decide as a nation to commit our sons and daughters to harm's way or keep them there for a decade. This method is fair.

- **Efficiency.** The combination of a change in the mix of active components and reserve components of our ground forces, the ARFORGEN model, and limited conscription into the reserve components creates an efficient and predictable method of manning the force. It provides a stable, sustainable force that is not subject to recruiting crises due to variations in unemployment rates, propensity to serve, or combat casualty rates. Finally, it provides Pentagon war planners and combatant commanders ready access to trained forces within thirty to forty-five days and the ability to sustain rotations in the desired 2:1 active-component and 5:1 reserve-component dwell time ratios. This reduces the incidence of PTSD, family stress, prescription psychotropic drug use, and other problems to which the violations of dwell-time policies have contributed. Skill sets conscripted into the force could also reduce the requirement for contractors, especially in areas like information technology, intelligence analysis, and language skills. It virtually eliminates the need to pay enlistment bonuses to incentivize recruits to join the reserve-component ground forces and allows the Army National Guard and Army Reserve to redeploy thousands of full-time recruiters to other roles.

- **Sustainability. From a fiscal standpoint, this alternative is sustainable, as it saves as much as $75 billion per year in**

personnel costs. These savings would also be augmented by the closure of certain military installations in foreign countries as the active force contracts from 490,000 to 290,000 members. It is further sustainable because the supply of Americans turning eighteen each year far exceeds the demand to man the reserve component at the recommended levels. The final question of sustainability rests with the American people and their leaders. Are we serious enough about the defense of our nation to require a small portion of our young citizens to provide two summers of their lives (one for basic training and the other for advanced individual training) and then one paid weekend per month and two paid weeks of annual training per year for six years (a total of 228 days)? Are we willing to embrace and sustain a system that causes every American family, rich or poor, liberal or conservative, Democrat or Republican, to have skin in the game?

The five alternatives are graphically presented in the matrix below:

	Fair	Efficient	Sustainable
National Service	Yes	No	No
UMT	Yes	No	No
Conscription	Yes	Yes	?*
AVF	No	No	No
Fifth Alternative	Yes	Yes	?*

*The sustainability of each of these alternatives is subject to the willingness of the American people to have skin in the game.

AFTERWORD

Now is the time to ask the question is the AVF working and will it work in the future. Tomorrow or in the middle of our next war is too late.

War is a horrible reality in the history of mankind. Inherent in its prosecution is death, destruction, suffering, and suspension of rational thinking. In most wars there are no winners—only those who lose less. All actors pay a huge price, and outcomes are unpredictable. In America's most recently concluded war in Iraq, there were no claims of victory from the White House or the Pentagon. In fact, the 2012 Army Posture Statement signed by both the secretary of the army and the army chief of staff, described the conclusion of the Iraq War by stating that "the mission in Iraq has ended responsibly." The word *win* was never used in reference to the war in the thirty-five page document, notwithstanding the heading "Prevent, Shape, Win." Critics might suggest that the only winners in the Iraq War were Iran, China, and Halliburton. Given the history of the American propensity to go to war, the current range of perceived threats to US national security, and American militarism, it is inevitable that the United States will go to war again in my lifetime.

The prosecution of war requires manpower. The purpose of this book is to engage the question of whether the current method of manning the American military, the AVF, is working and whether it will work in the future. Given what we have learned over the past twelve years of war and what we know of current trends in our society, can we expect to be able to man the force with high-quality recruits in the quantities required? Given the current state of our national finances and the trends in military personnel costs, can we afford to man the AVF?

Prior to 2001, the AVF benefitted from two developments not foreseen by its architects. The first was the collapse of the Soviet Empire, which allowed the United States to dramatically reduce the size of its military, thereby reducing the number of recruits required. All things being equal, it is easier to man a smaller force than a larger force. A similar gift is nowhere in sight today. The second development was the dramatic increase of women's participation in the military. In 1967, six years before the birth of the AVF, the participation of women was capped at 2 percent of the total force. Today, women represent almost 15 percent of the force. Whether this growth continues will be influenced by how effectively the military deals with sexual violence and combat exclusion rules.

Since 2001, the Pentagon has taken extraordinary measures to prosecute two long wars using a volunteer force that was never intended to be used in such a manner. The Pentagon chose to change or ignore some long-standing policies. It changed its policy regarding the use of psychotropic drugs to help service members deal with depression, anxiety, PTSD, and other emotional and mental health problems. It violated its policy regarding dwell times, sending service members back to war zones for third, fourth, and fifth tours with insufficient recovery periods. It lowered enlistment standards for high-school graduation, physical fitness, and moral rectitude. Finally, it ignored failures in physical fitness and weight control standards that would have led to discharge by regulation.

The Pentagon also chose to change practices to accommodate the shortcomings of the AVF concept. It paid unprecedented cash bonuses to enlistees to expand the pool of candidates. It expanded the use of civilian contractors to perform tasks traditionally performed by uniformed service members. It used stop-loss to retain service members against their will, generating charges of a backdoor draft inconsistent with the all-volunteer concept. It delayed or ignored the investigation or prosecution of discharges under DADT.

These and other changes in policies and practices to support the AVF concept have visited tragic consequences on service members and their families. They have also weakened the readiness, capabilities, and credibility of our national defense establishment. In summary, the AVF is not working and will not work in the future. It will collapse for one or both of two reasons: we will not be able to attract enough people who are both willing and able to enlist without dramatically lowering standards, or we will be unable to afford the personnel costs of the AVF. **In the interest of our own national security, it is imperative that we have an informed national dialogue regarding alternatives to the AVF that are fair, efficient, and sustainable. After Iraq and Afghanistan is an ideal time to engage this dialogue while the lessons learned are still clear in our minds. The alternative is to ask a different and more alarming question: What if we had a war and no one showed up on our side?**

APPENDIXES

Appendix 1

	#16 Iran	#29 North Korea	#3 China	#1 United States
Total Population	78,868,711	24,451,285	1,334,130,000	313,847,465
Available Manpower	46,247,556	12,933,972	749,610,775	145,212,012
Fit for Service	39,556,497	10,066,704	618,588,627	120,022,084
Active Military	545,000	1,106,000	2,285,000	1,477,896
Active Reserve	650,000	8,200,000	800,000	1,458,500
Tanks	2,895	5,400	7,950	8,325
Rocket Systems	860	1,600	2,600	1,330
Antitank Systems	11,400	17,000	31,250	28,000
Total Aircrafts	1,858	1,667	2,743	15,293
Ships	408	708	972	290
Carriers	0	0	1	10
Deficit Budget	$10.6 billion	$7.0 billion	$129 billion	$689.5 billion
Land Area	1.6 million km	120,000 km	9.5 million km	9.8 million km
Nuclear Capability	No	Yes	Yes	Yes

Appendix 2

From *Eliminating Major Gaps in DoD Data on the Fully Burdened and Life-Cycle Cost of Military Personnel: Cost Elements Should Be Mandated by Policy*

1. The cost of a reserve-component service member, when not activated, is less than one-third of that of his or her active-component counterpart. According to RFPB analysis of the fiscal year 2013 budget request, the reserve-components' per capita cost ranges from 22 percent to 32 percent of their active-component counterparts' per capita costs, depending on which cost elements are included.

2. While reserve component forces account for 39 percent of military end strength, they consume only about 16 percent of the defense budget.

3. Reserve-component members receive a smaller retirement than their active-component counterparts. The reserve components account for approximately 17 percent of DOD retiree payout. The fiscal year 2013 average retired pay accrual is $12,834 per active-component service member but only $3,419 per reserve-component service member.

4. Reserve-component members incur lower health-care costs. For fiscal year 2013, the DOD requested $32.5 billion for the Defense Health Program (plus nearly $8 billion in military medical personnel funds and nearly $7 billion in Medicare-eligible retiree health care accrual funds) to serve more than 9.5 million beneficiaries. Only about 21 percent of those beneficiaries are from the reserve components, and as a whole, reserve-component members use the system less than active-component members.

5. Reserve-component members serve in their home town and rarely incur military moving costs, for which the DOD requested $3,260 per active-component service member in fiscal year 2013.

6. With few exceptions, reserve families do not send dependent children to DOD schools, and only reservists serving on active duty are counted for Impact Aid calculations. For fiscal year 2013, the DOD Education Activity requested $2.7 billion, and the Department of Education's Impact Aid program requested $505 million. The project

team estimates that reservists account for approximately 1 percent of the DOD's and approximately 2 percent of the Department of Education's funds to educate military dependents.

7. Generally, reservists are ineligible to use the military family housing system, which required $1.3 billion to build and operate in fiscal year 2013. Only reservists on active-duty orders qualify for on-base housing, and few use it.

8. Reservists do not drive the need for military commissaries, which in fiscal year 2013 cost $1.37 billion over and above revenue income in order to operate. Only 3 percent of commissary users are from the reserve component.

9. Since the reserve component does not require as much infrastructure as the active component, it incurs a far lower cost for base operations support including maintenance, security, and utilities costs associated with the housing, childcare, and recreation facilities found on major bases. This is true whether the reservist is mobilized or in a drill status. Of the roughly $36 billion in DOD base operations support costs, about 12 percent is appropriated for reserve components.

10. Reservists account for a relatively small portion of the contributions made by the US Treasury over and above the DOD budget for defense-related costs.

    a. The US Treasury's direct contribution for concurrent receipt of both military retired pay and Veterans disability compensation was estimated at $ 6.95 billion for fiscal year 2013, but only 9 percent is attributable to reserve-component recipients.

    b. b. The US Treasury direct contribution for Medicare-Eligible Retiree Health Care Fund over and above the DOD contribution was estimated at $6.44 billion in fiscal year 2013, but only 29 percent of the liability for that cost is attributable to the reserve components.

    c. c. The US Treasury direct contribution to the Military Retirement Fund over and above the DOD contribution was estimated at $67.18 billion in fiscal year 2013, but only 17 percent of the payout from that fund is made to reserve-component retirees.

REFERENCES

1. Army Posture Statement. 2012.
2. "I Want You! The evolution of the All-Volunteer Force", Bernard Rostker, RAND Corporation, 2006.
3. "The Price of Civilization", Jeffrey D. Sachs, Random House, 2011.
4. "Immunity to Change", Robert Kegan and Lisa Laskow Lahey, Harvard Business Press, 2009
5. "The Real War", Richard Nixon, Simon and Schuster, 1980
6. "Generating Health & Discipline in the Force Ahead of Strategic Reset", Report 2012, Headquarters, Department of the Army.
7. "National Defense in a Time of Change", The Hamilton Project, Bookings Institution, February 2013.
8. "A Formula for Operational Capacity", Implementing the Army Force Generation Model in the Army National Guard, Army National Guard Directorate, 1 August 2011.
9. "Eliminating Major Gaps in DoD Data on the Fully-Burdened and Life-Cycle Cost of Military Personnel: Cost Elements Should Be Mandated By Policy", Reserve Force Policy Board, Final Report to the Secretary of Defense, January 7, 2013.
10. "The New American Militerism", Andrew J. Bacevich, Oxford University Press, 2005.
11. "Washington Rules", Andrew J. Bacevich, Metropolitan Books, Henry Holt and Company, 2010.

12. "Strategic Vision", Zbigniew Brzezinski, Basic Books, 2012.

13. "Three Trillion Dollar War", Joseph E. Stinglitz and Linda J. Bilmes, W.W. Norton & Company, 2008.

14. "Are We Rome, The Fall of an Empire and the Fate of America", Cullen Murphy, First Mariner Books, 2007.

15. "AWOL: The Unexcused Absence of America's Upper Classes from Military service—and How It Hurts Our Country", Kathy Roth Douquet and Frank Schaeffer, HarperCollins Books, 2006.

16. "National Priorities Project: Military Recruitment 2010", June 30, 2011.

INDEX